D0605185

Rodale's Treasury of Christmas Crafts

Christmas Bazaar

Rodale's Treasury of Christmas Crafts

Christmas Bazaar

Rodale Press, Emmaus, Pennsylvania

Our Mission

We publish books that empower people's lives.

RODALE BOOKS

Rodale Press Staff

Executive Editor
Margaret Lydic Balitas

Copy Editor
Carolyn R. Mandarano

Editors
Karen Bolesta
Nancy Reames

Book Designer
Patricia Field

Photography
Mitch Mandel, pages 41, 62, 74, 84, 109, 120

If you have any questions or comments concerning this book, please write to:

Rodale Press, Inc.
Book Readers' Service
33 East Minor Street
Emmaus PA 18098

Printed in the United States of America
Published by Rodale Press, Inc.
Distributed in the book trade by St. Martin's Press

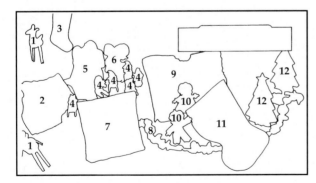

Projects on Cover: (1) Scent of Cinnamon Ornaments,
(2) Purrfectly Pretty Sweatshirt, (3) Holiday Magic
Embroidered Stockings, (4) Tiny Town Christmas Troupe,
(5) Swinging Star Angel, (6) Holiday Handkerchief Angel,
(7) Christmas Comfort Appliquéd Pillows, (8) Fruits and
Treasures Garland, (9) Beribboned Pillow, (10) Stocking Stuffer
Dolls, (11) Santa's Reindeer Stocking and (12) Little Tree Clocks

For Chapelle Ltd.

Owners
Terrece Beesley and Jo Packham

Staff

Trice Boerens
Tina Annette Brady
Gaylene Byers
Sheri Lynn Castle
Holly Fuller
Cherie Hanson
Susan Jorgensen
Margaret Shields Marti

Jackie McCowen
Barbara Milburn
Pamela Randall
Jennifer Roberts
Florence Stacey
Nancy Whitley
Gloria Zirkel

Photography
Ryne Hazen

Book Design, Project Design and Text
Chapelle Ltd., Ogden, Utah 84401   © 1993 by Chapelle Ltd.

The photographs in this book were taken at Trends and Traditions, Ogden, Utah; Bloomingsales, Salt Lake City, Utah; and at the homes of Bonnie Galbraith, Ogden, Utah; Penelope Hammons, Layton, Utah, and Jo Packham, Ogden, Utah. Their trust and cooperation are deeply appreciated.

The author and editors who compiled this book have tried to make all of the contents as accurate and as correct as possible. Graphs, illustrations, photographs and text have all been carefully checked and cross-checked. However, due to the variability of local conditions, tools and supplies, personal skill and so on, Rodale Press assumes no responsibility for any injuries suffered or for damages or other losses incurred that result from the material presented herein. All instructions should be carefully studied and clearly understood before beginning a project.

Library of Congress Cataloging-in-Publication Data
Christmas bazaar.
      p.   cm. -- (Rodale's treasury of Christmas crafts)
    ISBN 0–87596–598–9 hardcover
    1. Christmas decorations. 2. Handicraft. I. Rodale Press.
II. Series.
TT900 . C4C433   1993
745 . 594 ' 12--dc20

                                      93–8108
                                        CIP

2 4 6 8 10 9 7 5 3 1 hardcover

ontents

$\mathcal{S}$anta's Reindeer Stocking

Trimmed with buttons and satin stitching, this happy reindeer bounds past a row of evergreen trees on his way to pull Santa's sleigh!

MATERIALS

⅝ yard of green print fabric; matching thread
Scrap of green felt; matching thread
⅜ yard of red felt; matching thread
¼ yard of paper-backed fusible webbing
Tracing paper
⅜ yard of fusible tear-away
Dressmaker's pen
⅛ yard of ½"-wide green ribbon
Sixteen small, white buttons

DIRECTIONS

1. Enlarge stocking pattern on page 9; see "General Instructions" on page 126. From red felt, cut two stockings. From tear-away, cut one stocking. For stocking lining pattern, add 2" to top of stocking pattern to allow for faux cuff. From green print fabric, cut two lining pieces. Also from green print fabric, cut 2"-wide bias strips, piecing as needed to equal 1½ yards of binding; set aside.

2. From green felt and fusible webbing, cut one 12" x 12" piece each. Fuse rough side of webbing to felt.

3. Trace reindeer pattern on page 8. Trace antler pattern; set aside. Trace tree pattern on page 8. Transfer reindeer and three trees to paper side of green felt. Cut out. Remove paper.

4. Position trees, webbing side down, on right side of stocking front, with bottom edges 5" from stocking top; see photo. Fuse to felt. Position reindeer on stocking front as desired; see photo. Fuse to felt. Place shiny side of tear-away stocking against wrong side of appliquéd stocking. Iron.

5. Using green thread, finish edges of appliqués with machine satin stitching. Using dressmaker's pen, transfer antler pattern to stocking above reindeer head. Machine satin-stitch antlers. To remove tear-away, lift at one corner and carefully tear. To remove from appliqués, make a small scissor cut in portion of tear-away backing appliqués; lift and tear.

6. Mark line 1¾" below and parallel to top edge of both felt stocking pieces. With right sides facing, layer one stocking piece and one lining piece, matching top edge of lining to marked line. Stitch ¼" from lining edge. Repeat with remaining stocking and lining pieces. Fold lining pieces to back side of stocking pieces. Layer stocking back, then front, matching all edges. Pin edges together.

7. With right sides facing, sew binding to stocking front, using ½" seam and folding ends under at top edge. Fold binding to stocking back and slipstitch, covering stitching line.

8. Sew buttons to stocking front as desired; see photo. For hanger, make loop with green ribbon. Tack inside top of stocking back on heel side.

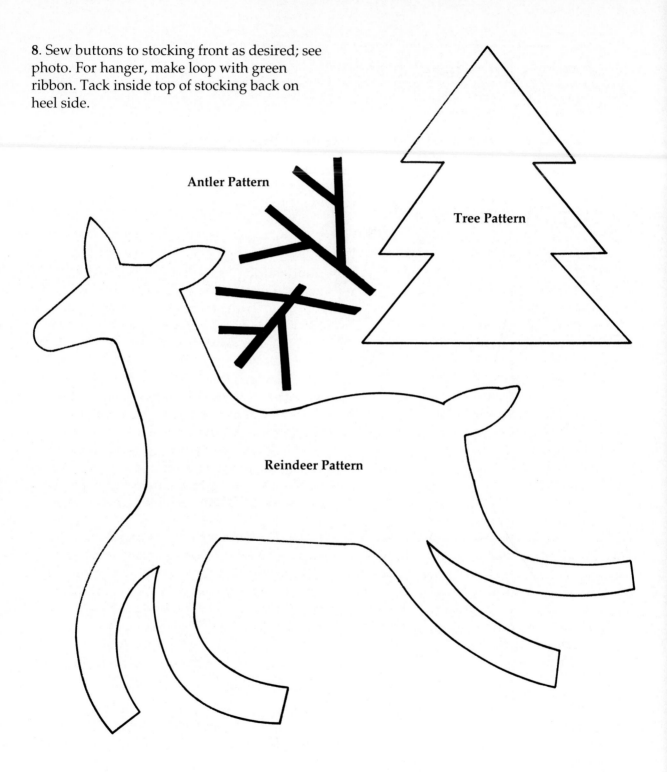

Antler Pattern

Tree Pattern

Reindeer Pattern

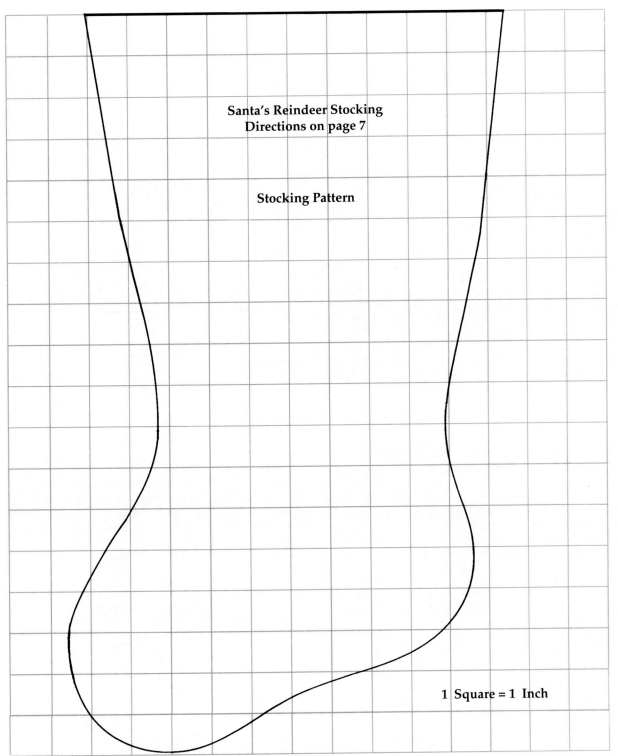

Santa's Reindeer Stocking
Directions on page 7

Stocking Pattern

1 Square = 1 Inch

Fruits and Treasures Garland

You decide the look and aroma of this delightful garland, then ornament your tree or some other special spot. Make it in minutes; enjoy it all season!

MATERIALS

Tan pearl cotton
Large-eyed needle
Dried limes, oranges, artichokes, corn kernels
Cinnamon sticks
Assorted nuts
Bay leaves
Small pinecones
Small wooden cutouts: hearts, blocks, disks
Miniature baskets
Miniature bird nests
Wooden beads
Drill with ¹⁄₁₆" drill bit

Note: Other dried fruits, miniature cookie-cutters, tiny fabric hearts or any other natural-looking miniature may be substituted for materials listed.

DIRECTIONS

1. Gather enough fruits, wooden cutouts, beads, nuts and assorted miniatures to fill a 3' length of pearl cotton. To make a longer garland, join 3' segments to equal desired length. Drill ¹⁄₁₆"-wide holes in nuts, wooden cutouts and any other items which may be difficult to pierce with a needle.

2. Cut a 50" length of pearl cotton. Thread end through eye of needle. To string garland, pass needle through first garland item and pull item onto pearl cotton. Continue stringing, pulling each item back snugly to make room for additional items as needed. Knot ends of pearl cotton when garland is complete.

Try This

Use a small garland to decorate the rim of a woven basket. Secure the ends of pearl cotton through the basket weave at the rim, or around the basket handle. Use lengths of pearl cotton at intervals along the garland to secure it to the basket rim through the weave. Fill the basket with fruits, potpourri, evergreen foliage or silk flowers.

To dry citrus fruit, cut into ¼"-thick slices. To keep the bright color, dip each slice into liquid fruit preservative (available at supermarkets). Place slices 1" apart on cooling rack. Place rack on cookie sheet. Leave overnight in oven set at 150°F or on "warm" setting.

$\mathcal{B}$eribboned Pillow

A rummage through your scrap basket creates a unique design in ribbon, braid and trim. You'll want several of these handsome, one-of-a-kind pillows.

MATERIALS

Two 17½" black chintz squares; matching thread
1¼ yards of red chintz; matching thread
2 yards of large cording
8–10 yards of assorted ribbon, braid, trim
Polyester stuffing

DIRECTIONS
All seams are ¼".

1. From red chintz, cut 2¼"-wide bias strips, piecing as needed to equal 2 yards. Cover cording with pieced bias strips; see "General Instructions" on page 126 for corded piping.

2. To make pillow front, topstitch lengths of ribbon, braid and trim in sections to one black chintz square to create desired pattern. Place finished edges of ribbon, braid or trim lengths parallel to, but not over, previous lengths. See diagram for suggested groupings. Place raw ends under overlapping lengths. Keep adding groupings until the chintz is covered.

3. With right sides facing and raw edges aligned, sew corded piping to pillow front.

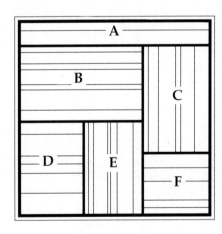

Diagram

With right sides facing, sew pillow front to pillow back along stitching line of piping, leaving an opening. Turn. Stuff firmly. Slipstitch opening closed.

Glass Greetings Decoupaged Plates

If you've been saving pretty Christmas cards and pictures, you can use them now to create a set of one-of-a-kind holiday plates. Thrift-store plates work just fine!

MATERIALS (for one)

One clear glass dinner or serving plate
Christmas carol sheet music
Christmas pictures from magazines
Old Christmas cards
Scissors
Decoupage glue and glue brush
Acrylic paint: black
Paintbrush

DIRECTIONS

1. Trim magazine pictures as desired. From Christmas cards, cut out desired motifs. Save one or two pictures or motifs about 5" tall for center of plate; set aside. To make border around edge of plate, arrange remaining pictures and motifs face up under plate and slightly overlapping. Trim top edges of border items to fit plate edge. Trim bottom edges to make circle around center of plate.

2. Using decoupage glue and glue brush, apply glue to right side of one picture or motif at a time. Smooth each item onto plate in desired position. Allow some drying time for each item before applying another.

3. Position 5"-tall pictures or motifs as desired in center of plate. Apply glue to right sides of pictures or motifs. Smooth onto center of plate in desired position.

4. From sheet music, cut a circle to fit center of plate, slightly overlapping bottom edges of border items; clip curves. Apply glue to right side of sheet music piece. Smooth onto center of plate, over large pictures or motifs. Allow glue to dry completely.

5. Paint back of plate black. Allow to dry completely.

6. Clean plates by sponging off unpainted side, rinsing with damp sponge or cloth and immediately drying with a paper towel. Decoupaged plates should not be submerged in water.

Try This

Create sets of themed plates by using all Santa Claus cutouts, all Christmas sheet music, all snow scenes or other seasonal groupings. Or add a family photo in the center for a personalized look.

To make purely decorative plates, glue beads or plastic holly sprigs around rim of each and place in plate stand or hanger.

$\mathcal{G}$reat North Woods Stocking

The ideal stocking to decorate the den for the holidays!

MATERIALS (for one 14" x 22" stocking)

⅜ yard of tan wool;
   black thread
⅜ yard of green tweed
Tracing paper
Brown pearl cotton
   size 5
Large-eyed needle
¼ yard of burgundy
   wool
9" x 9" piece of paper-
   backed fusible webbing

¼ yard of polyester
   sheepskin;
   matching thread
Six buttons
¼ yard of ⅜"-wide
   brown ribbon

DIRECTIONS

All seams are ¼".

1. Enlarge pattern for stocking top and foot on page 19; see "General Instructions" on page 126. Trace reindeer pattern on page 18, transferring all information. From tan wool, cut two stocking tops. From green tweed, cut two feet.

2. With right sides facing, sew one top to one foot according to pattern. Press seams open. Repeat with remaining top and foot. With wrong sides facing, sew tops together with black thread, leaving top of stocking open and feet unstitched. Baste feet. Using brown pearl cotton and large-eyed needle, sew feet together with buttonhole stitch; see diagram.

3. Transfer reindeer pattern to paper side of fusible webbing. Fuse rough side of webbing to wrong side of burgundy wool. Cut out appliqué. Remove paper. Center horizontally on stocking front with feet on green tweed; see photo. Fuse.

4. From sheepskin, cut one 5" x 22" piece for cuff. With wrong sides facing, sew short ends together, using a running stitch. Slide cuff over stocking, aligning top edges and seams. Sew top edge of cuff to stocking, using a running stitch.

5. Sew buttons to stocking front along stitching line; see photo. To make hanger, cut one 6" length of brown ribbon. Make loop and tack hanger inside top edge of stocking on heel side.

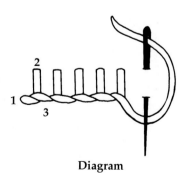

Diagram

Reindeer Pattern

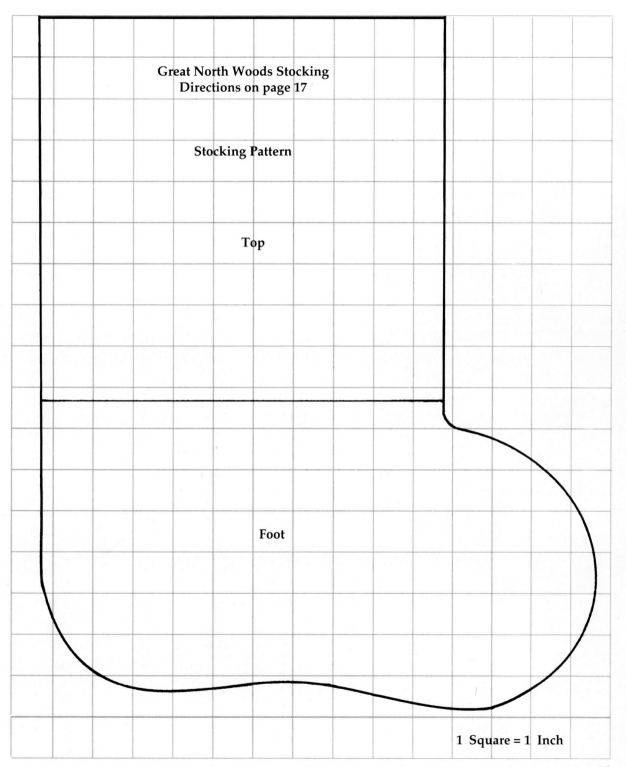

Great North Woods Stocking
Directions on page 17

Stocking Pattern

Top

Foot

1 Square = 1 Inch

Reason for the Season Nativity Set

This simply constructed nativity set expresses the true meaning of a special time of year. Display it with evergreens and votive candles for a striking centerpiece.

MATERIALS (for Mary)

Tracing paper
Craft knife
¼ yard of blue print fabric; matching thread
6¼" x 10¼" piece of burgundy fabric;
  matching thread
Scrap of light pink fabric
Scrap of mat board
1 cup of plastic beads
Polyester stuffing
Black and cranberry red felt-tip markers
Pink blusher
Hot glue gun and glue sticks
¼ yard of dark brown braided wool roving
½ yard of gold cord
Metallic gold thread
Dressmaker's pen

DIRECTIONS
All seams are ¼".

1. Trace patterns for head, body, sleeves, arms, bottom and base on pages 25–26, transferring all information. From blue fabric, cut one body, one bottom and one sleeve piece. From pink fabric, cut one head and two arms. Transfer pattern for base to mat board. Cut one base.

2. With right sides facing, sew center back seam of body from bottom edge up to dot on pattern; back tack. With right sides facing, sew bottom to lower edge of body. Turn.

3. Insert base in bottom so it lies flat. Add plastic beads for balance. Stuff remainder of body firmly. Slipstitch remainder of center back seam closed, leaving neck open.

4. Fold fabric under ¼" along edge of head piece. Sew gathering thread near fold; gather loosely. Stuff head firmly. Tighten thread and secure. Turn raw edge of body under ¼". Place head on body, with gathered side inside neck. Slipstitch head securely to body, gathering neck as needed. With felt-tip marker, add details to face, using black for eyes and cranberry for nose and mouth. Apply pink blusher to cheeks.

5. For hair, cut braided roving into short lengths; fluff. Glue to head as desired.

6. With right sides facing, sew edges of one arm, leaving end opposite hand open. Fold fabric under ¼" at open end. Repeat with second arm. Sew gathering thread loosely at each open end near fold; do not cut thread. Stuff arms firmly.

7. Hem each end of sleeve piece. With right sides facing, sew together unhemmed edges; turn. Insert small amount of stuffing in center of sleeve piece according to pattern. Place open end of one arm inside each sleeve. Tack arms to inside of sleeves.

8. Securely tack sleeve piece with arms to center back seam of body, making sure seam is down. Slipstitch in place for 1½" along each side of body, bending arms forward.

9. To make mantle, hem burgundy fabric. Knot ends of gold cord. Position mantle on head as desired; see photo. Wrap gold cord snugly around top of head, allowing tails to hang down in back and easing fullness of burgundy fabric. Pin or baste.

10. Using gold thread, tack cord to head. Wrap thread around cord tails, securing thread ends in cord knots.

¼ yard of auburn braided wool roving
½ yard of burgundy cord
Metallic gold thread
Dressmaker's pen

DIRECTIONS
All seams are ¼".

1. Repeat Steps 1–8 for Mary, using cream/red fabric for body, sleeves and bottom. Use auburn braided roving for hair and beard. To make mantle, repeat Step 9 for Mary, using cream fabric and burgundy cord.

MATERIALS (for one Wise Man)

Tracing paper
Craft knife
¼ yard of multicolored print fabric
6½" x 10¼" piece of silk or polyester
Scrap of light pink, beige or brown fabric
Scrap of mat board
1 cup of plastic beads
Polyester stuffing
Black and cranberry red felt-tip markers
Pink blusher
Hot glue gun and glue sticks
¼ yard of cream, gray or black
  braided wool roving
¾ yard of ⅜"-wide flat gold trim
1 yard of ¼"-wide flat gold trim
Scrap of gold cardboard
Mock jewel(s)

MATERIALS (for Joseph)

Tracing paper
Craft knife
¼ yard cream/red fabric; matching thread
6¼" x 10¼" piece of cream fabric;
  matching thread
Scrap of light pink fabric
Scrap of mat board
1 cup of plastic beads
Polyester stuffing
Black and cranberry red felt-tip markers
Pink blusher
Hot glue gun and glue sticks

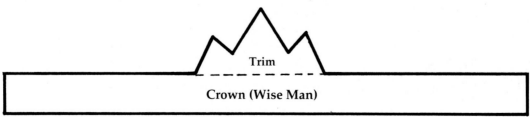

Trim

Crown (Wise Man)

DIRECTIONS

All seams are ¼".

1. Repeat Steps 1–8 for Mary, using multi-colored fabric for body, sleeves and bottom and light pink, beige or brown fabric for head and arms. Use cream, gray or black braided roving for hair and beard.

2. Trace pattern for crown on page 22. Mark and cut two crowns from gold cardboard; set aside.

3. To finish body, cut ⅜"-wide trim into two 5" lengths and one 16" length. Glue one 5" length around end of each sleeve, trimming excess. Start 16" length at top of body on front, to one side of center. Glue down center front of body, around bottom edge and back up front to opposite side of center; see photo.

4. To make mantle, hem edges of silk. Glue ¼"-wide gold trim along edges on right side of fabric. Position mantle on head. Gathering silk loosely, stitch to head. Tighten thread; secure. To finish crown, glue two crowns together with wrong sides facing. Glue ends of crown together. Glue crown to head, covering stitches in mantle. To make a flat crown, use same crown pattern and trim off points. Glue jewels to crown as desired; see photo.

MATERIALS (for Baby Jesus)

Tracing paper
Scrap of cream chintz; matching thread
Scrap of light pink fabric
Polyester stuffing
⅜ yard of ⅛"-wide beige ribbon
Black and cranberry red felt-tip markers
Dressmaker's pen
Pink blusher

DIRECTIONS

All seams are ¼".

1. Trace patterns for head on page 26 and bunting front and bunting back on page 25, transferring all information. From chintz, cut one bunting front and one bunting back. From light pink fabric, cut one head.

2. Turn fabric under ¼" around edge of head piece. Sew gathering thread near fold. Gather loosely. Stuff head firmly. Tighten thread and secure. With felt-tip marker, add details to face, using black for eyes and cranberry for nose and mouth. Apply pink blusher to cheeks.

3. Turn fabric under ¼" at narrow end of bunting front. Sew gathering thread near fold; do not cut thread. With right sides facing, stitch bunting front to back, leaving top open. Turn. Sew gathering thread around curved edge of bunting back, ¼" from edge; do not cut thread. Stuff bunting moderately. Insert head with gathered end to back. Tighten gathering threads of bunting back and front snugly around head; secure. Tack gathers to head.

4. Find center of ribbon and place at back of neck. Bring each ribbon end to one side of neck. Cross ends over chest and over bottom edge of bunting. Cross ends at back of head, wrapping to front, then to back. Knot ends in back of head; trim.

MATERIALS (for manger)

Small cardboard tissue tube
Tape
Hot glue gun and glue sticks
Ten 3½"-long whole cinnamon sticks

23

Four 2½"-long whole cinnamon sticks
½ yard of jute
Handful of straw

DIRECTIONS

1. Tape tube to work surface. Using tube as a form, glue together longer cinnamon sticks, shaping to form a moderate V.

2. Cut jute into two 9" lengths. For manger supports, cross two shorter cinnamon sticks and glue. Using crisscross pattern, wrap one length around each set of manger supports. Knot ends and trim. Glue one set of supports ¼" in from each end of manger.

3. Turn manger right side up. Glue straw inside. Place Baby Jesus in manger.

Try This

Nativity set figures may also be filled with fragrant potpourri in place of the polyester stuffing.

Add small wooden or stuffed animals to the scene. A backdrop may be created by gluing twigs together in an upright position on one edge of a piece of mat board large enough to hold all the figures. Glue a bright Christmas star made of gold or silver foil to the backdrop and glue more straw to the "floor" before positioning the figures.

**Bunting Front
(Baby Jesus)**

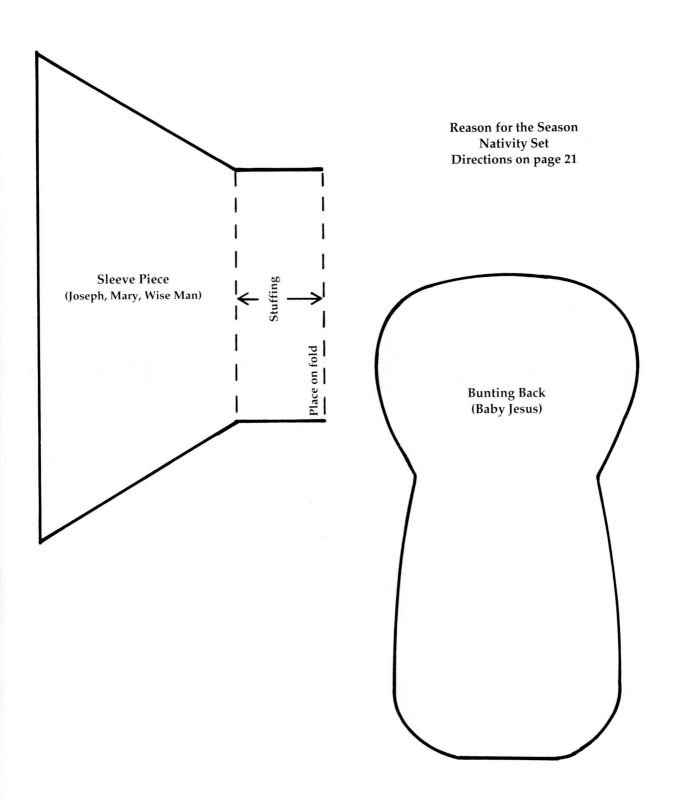

Sleeve Piece
(Joseph, Mary, Wise Man)

Stuffing

Place on fold

Reason for the Season
Nativity Set
Directions on page 21

Bunting Back
(Baby Jesus)

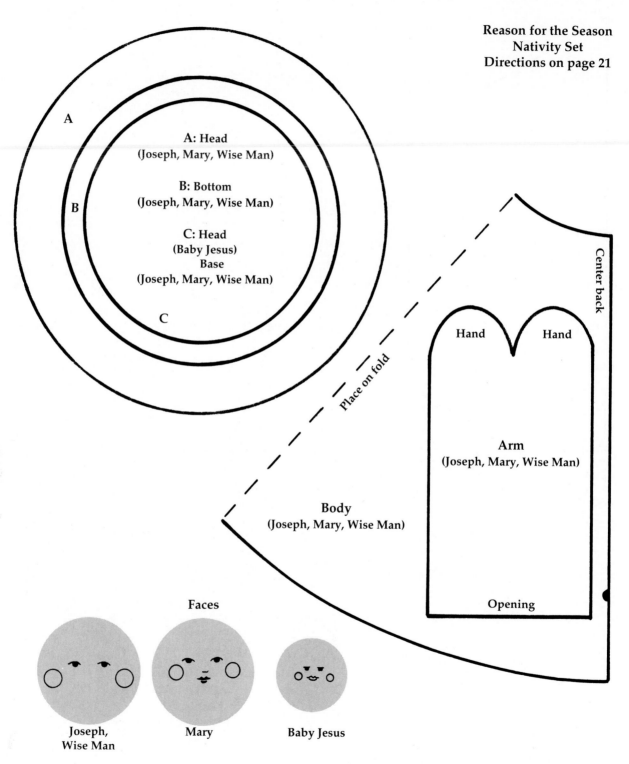

Reason for the Season
Nativity Set
Directions on page 21

A

A: Head
(Joseph, Mary, Wise Man)

B: Bottom
(Joseph, Mary, Wise Man)

B

C: Head
(Baby Jesus)
Base
(Joseph, Mary, Wise Man)

C

Place on fold

Center back

Hand   Hand

Arm
(Joseph, Mary, Wise Man)

Body
(Joseph, Mary, Wise Man)

Opening

Faces

Joseph,
Wise Man

Mary

Baby Jesus

Opposite: Grandma's Little Christmas Stockings

Grandma's Little Christmas Stockings

Decorated with lace and other pretty things, these old-fashioned stockings recall the children's hose of another day. Fill them with small holiday treasures! (Project pictured on page 27.)

MATERIALS (for seven stockings)

1⅛ yards of off-white 1 x 1 cotton ribbing; matching thread
Tracing paper
Assorted tan and off-white tatted lace and crochet scraps
Assorted off-white buttons
Assorted tan buttons
Assorted tiny brown shells

DIRECTIONS
All seams are ¼".

1. Trace stocking pattern on page 29. From ribbing, cut out fourteen stocking shapes.

2. With right sides facing, sew stocking fronts to stocking backs, leaving top edges open. Serge or zigzag-stitch top edge of each stocking. Turn top edge of each stocking under ¾"; slipstitch.

3. Cut seven 4"-long scraps of tatted lace for hangers. Fold each, matching long edges. Tack one hanger on heel-side seam at top edge of each stocking. Clip stocking curves. Turn.

4. To complete stockings, embellish with crochet scraps, lace and buttons as desired. To attach shells, use needle to poke a hole in each shell before stitching it to stocking.

Try This

Stocking tops can also be embellished with sprigs of fresh holly or mistletoe. Fill the stockings with small candies, let a name card peep from each top and use as dinner-party place markers!

Stockings can also be dyed with natural materials such as brewed coffee or tea, cranberry juice or grape juice. Before decorating, allow each stocking to soak for three to four minutes in the desired liquid. Pat dry between paper towels. Place between two cotton rags and iron until fabric is dry. Colors will be soft and subtle when dry. Then decorate stockings as desired.

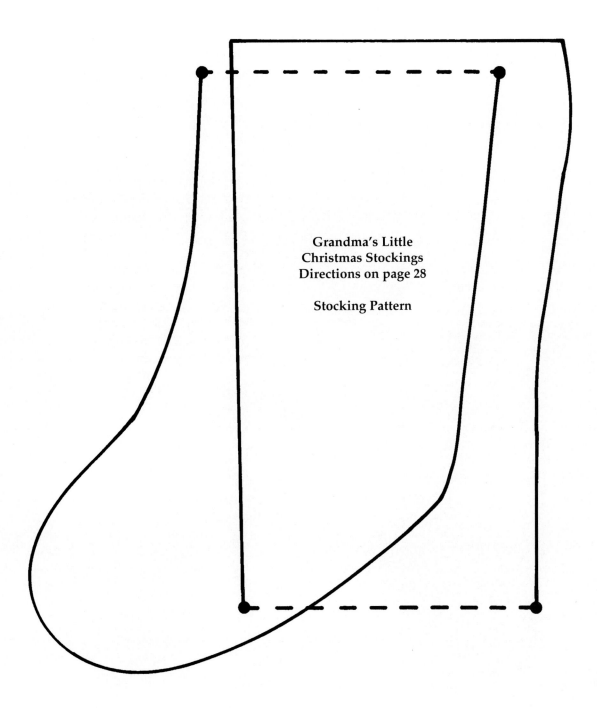

Grandma's Little
Christmas Stockings
Directions on page 28

Stocking Pattern

Mr. and Mrs. Snow

They're as soft as new-fallen snow and wear their Christmas best. They're easy and inexpensive to make, too!

MATERIALS (for Mrs. Snow)

Two pieces of 22" x 54" batting
White cord
Hot glue gun and glue sticks
Two large, black wooden beads
Three small red and green wooden beads
Two twigs
One 1"-diameter x 3"-long Styrofoam cone
Craft knife
Acrylic paint: orange
Miniature red straw hat with 5" opening
Dried leaves and cranberries
Two small pinecones
17" x 17" piece of green print fabric

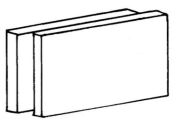

Diagram 1

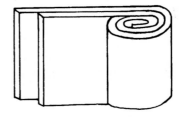

Diagram 2

DIRECTIONS

1. Layer two pieces of batting, offsetting ends; see Diagram 1. Handling as one, roll snugly into a tube; see Diagram 2.

2. Cut three 24" lengths of cord. Stand tube on end. To make waist, tie one length of cord snugly around tube, 11" from bottom. To make neck, tie cord around tube 5" above first cord. Secure top of tube with cord tied 1½" below top. Roll 2" of batting to inside of tube on lower edge to form curved shape; glue in place.

3. Using craft knife, shape Styrofoam cone into carrot. Paint orange. Allow to dry. Glue to face for nose. Glue black beads to face for eyes. Glue red and green beads to chest for buttons. Glue twigs to body for arms.

4. To decorate hat, glue on leaves, cranberries and pinecones in a cluster; see photo. Glue hat on head.

5. To make apron, cut green fabric in half diagonally. Pull threads along two short edges to make fringe. Turn unfringed edge under. Tie apron around waist.

MATERIALS (for Mr. Snow)

Two pieces of 22" x 54" batting
White cord
Hot glue gun and glue sticks
Two large, black wooden beads
Three small mock agate stones (available at
   craft stores)
Two twigs
One 1"-diameter x 3"-long Styrofoam cone
Craft knife
Acrylic paint: orange
Miniature top hat with 5" opening
⅛ yard of plaid wool

DIRECTIONS

1. Repeat Steps 1–3 for Mrs. Snow, using mock
agates for buttons.

2. Glue hat to head.

3. To make muffler, trim wool to 36" length.
Pull threads on each end to make fringe. Fold,
matching long edges. Tie around neck.

— *Try This* —

These batting figures can be dressed in
any style you like! You can create elegant
figures by dressing Mrs. Snow in brocade
and using roving to build a fancy hairstyle.
Dress Mr. Snow in formal wear, with a
black silk bow tie and rhinestone buttons.

Make a Country Snow family by using
gingham or bandannas for clothing and
baby-size knit caps.

Opposite: Small Wonder Stockings

mall Wonder Stockings

Tiny cross-stitched stockings make lovely ornaments or the perfect place to stash a special little gift of jewelry or money. (Project pictured on page 33.)

MODELS

Stitched on oatmeal Floba 25 over two threads, the finished design size is 3⅜" x 5" for each stocking. The fabric was cut 8" x 8".

FABRICS	DESIGN SIZES
Aida 11	3⅞" x 5¾"
Aida 14	3" x 4½"
Aida 18	2⅜" x 3½"
Hardanger 22	1⅞" x 2⅞"

Anchor   **DMC (used for sample)**

Step 1: Cross-stitch (2 strands)

Anchor		DMC	
20	- /	498	Christmas Red-dk.
879	O /	890	Pistachio Green-ultra dk.

Step 2: Stocking pattern

MATERIALS (for one stocking)

Completed design piece on oatmeal Floba
¼ yard of burgundy or forest green fabric; matching thread
⅜ yard of ⅛"-wide cording

DIRECTIONS

All seams are ¼".

1. Transfer heavy black line from graph on page 35 to completed stocking. Trim design piece ¼" outside of pen line. Using design piece as pattern, cut out three stockings from matching fabric for stocking back and lining. Also cut one ¾" x 5" strip for hanger and 1¼"-wide bias strips, piecing as need to equal ⅜ yard. Cover cording with pieced bias strips;

see "General Instructions" on page 126 for corded piping.

2. With right sides facing and raw edges aligned, sew piping to design piece. With right sides facing, sew design piece to stocking back along stitching line of piping, leaving top open. Clip curves and turn.

3. With wrong sides facing, fold fabric strip in half, matching long edges. Sew. Turn. Make loop. Baste hanger inside top of stocking back near back seam.

4. To make lining, sew together remaining stockings with right sides facing, leaving top open and an opening in seam above heel. Slide lining over stocking, aligning top edges and seams. Sew around top, securing hanger in seam. Turn through opening in lining. Slipstitch opening closed. Tuck lining inside stocking.

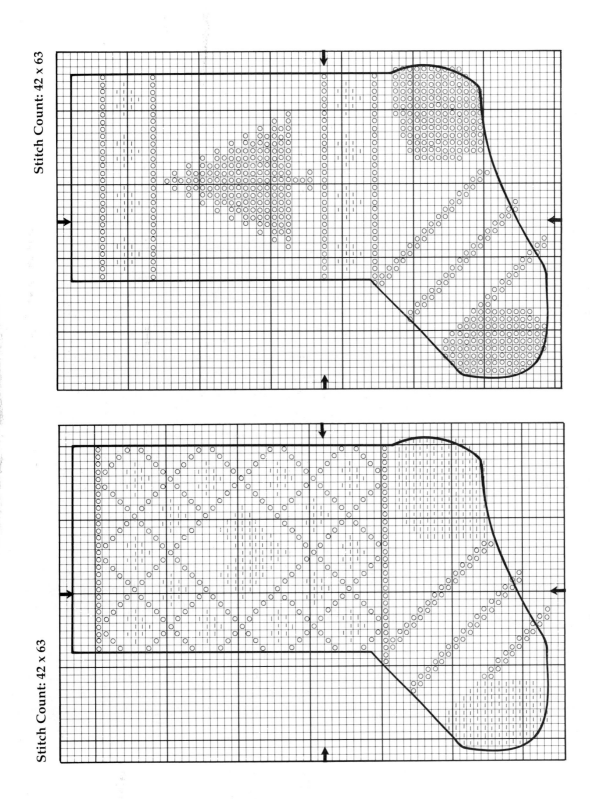

Stitch Count: 42 x 63

Stitch Count: 42 x 63

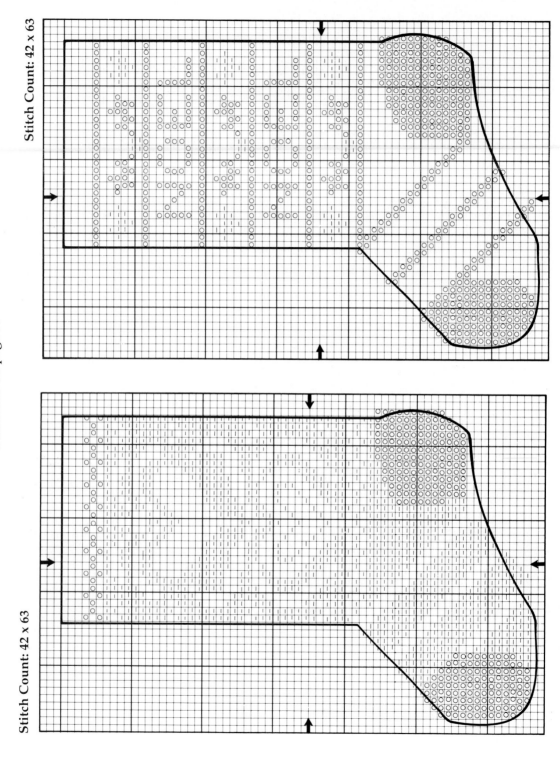

Small Wonder Stockings Graphs
Directions on page 34

Stitch Count: 42 x 63

Stitch Count: 42 x 63

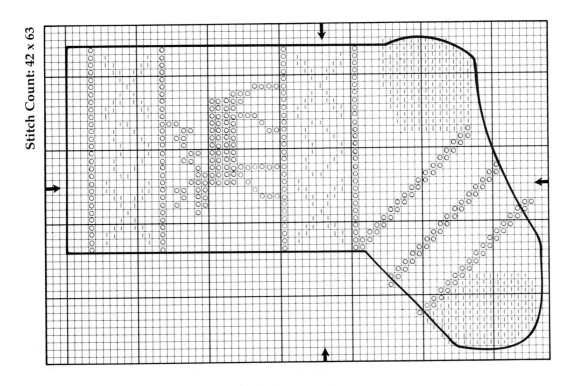

Stitch Count: 42 x 63

Small Wonder Stockings Graph
Directions on page 34

Anchor **DMC (used for sample)**

Step 1: Cross-stitch (2 strands)   **Step 2:** Stocking pattern

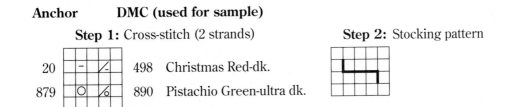

| 20 | − | ⁄ | 498 | Christmas Red-dk. |
| 879 | O | ⁄ | 890 | Pistachio Green-ultra dk. |

$\mathcal{A}$pples 'n' Spice Potpourri Pie

Apples and spice and all things nice are the recipe for this fragrant potpourri pie. Its delicate ribbon crust looks good enough to eat and smells heavenly!

MATERIALS

One 16-ounce bag of apple-cinnamon
  potpourri
One 8" aluminum pie pan
One 16-ounce bag of dried apple chips
Hot glue gun and glue sticks
12" x 12" square of white tulle netting
2½ yards of ⅞" cream ribbon
2½ yards of ½" cream ribbon
Sixty-nine red seed beads
12" x 12" square of sheer tricot
¼ cup of clear glitter
¼ cup of copper-colored glitter
Paper cup
Spray adhesive
Small dried tree branch
12" x 12" scrap of ⅛"-thick wood
Jigsaw
Acrylic paints: black, yellow, white
Paintbrush
Cinnamon stick

DIRECTIONS

1. Place potpourri in pie pan, spreading evenly. Cover with a layer of apple chips, mounding chips slightly in middle of pan. Reserve two apple chips for decoration.

2. Center netting over pan. Glue to flat rim. Trim excess flush with outer edge of rim.

3. Fold tricot in fourths to find center, then fold in half diagonally to form triangle. Cut 2" slit through all layers on long side of triangle. Repeat on opposite folded edge; see Diagram 1. Center tricot over pan. Glue to flat rim. Trim excess flush with outer edge of rim.

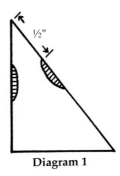

Diagram 1

4. Cut one 2¼-yard length of ⅞" ribbon and one 2¼-yard length of ½" ribbon. Glue ½" ribbon lengthwise along center of ⅞" ribbon. With ½" ribbon up, make and pin ½" box pleats along length of ribbons. Sew along center to secure pleats; see Diagram 2.

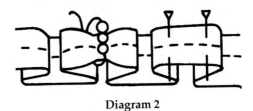

Diagram 2

5. Pinch center of each box pleat together. Sew three red seed beads to center of each box pleat; see Diagram 2. Glue pleated, beaded ribbon around rim of pie pan for "crust"; trim excess and tuck ends under.

6. In paper cup, mix clear and copper-colored glitter to desired color. Cover surface of pie with a light coating of spray adhesive. Sprinkle glitter mixture over sprayed area. Gently tap pie pan to remove excess.

7. Cut through netting inside one tricot slit cutout. Place bead of glue on end of tree branch. Insert end of branch through slit and potpourri; glue to bottom of pan.

8. Trace bird and wing patterns. Transfer to 12" x 12" wooden scrap, making seven birds and fourteen wings. Using a jigsaw, cut out birds and wings.

9. Paint both sides of each bird and wing black. Allow to dry. Paint beaks yellow and eyes white. Allow to dry. Glue two wings on each bird. Glue birds to branch and to pie as desired; see photo. Using glue, garnish middle of pie with reserved apple chips and cinnamon stick.

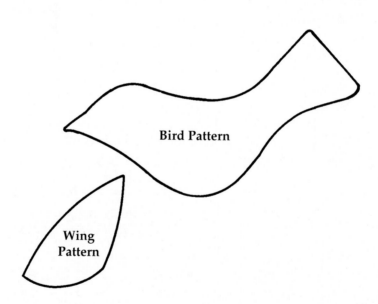

Bird Pattern

Wing Pattern

Opposite: Purrfectly Pretty Sweatshirt

$\mathscr{P}$urrfectly Pretty Sweatshirt

A pretty kitty and a garland of poinsettias create a delightful holiday design on a cozy, comfy sweatshirt. It's easy and fun to stitch! (Project pictured on page 41.)

MODEL (as shown)

Stitched over Waste Canvas 10* on a purchased white sweatshirt, the finished design size is 9¾" x 7¾". See directions before stitching. The graph is on page 43.

*See "Suppliers" on page 128.

DIRECTIONS

1. Cut Waste Canvas 1" larger than finished design size. Baste Waste Canvas to front of sweatshirt. Center design and begin stitching top of cat's ear 3" below neck seam of sweatshirt. Each stitch is over one unit (two threads).

When stitching is complete, use spray bottle to dampen stitched area with cold water. Pull Waste Canvas threads out one at a time with tweezers. It is easier to pull all horizontal threads first; then pull vertical threads. Allow stitching to dry, then place it facedown on a towel and iron.

Anchor		DMC (used for sample)	
Step 1: Cross-stitch (5 strands)			
891	−	676	Old Gold-lt.
868	∴	758	Terra Cotta-lt.
8	•	761	Salmon-lt.
10	✕	3712	Salmon-med.
214	△	368	Pistachio Green-lt.
215	▲	320	Pistachio Green-med.
398	○	415	Pearl Gray
401	■	413	Pewter Gray-dk.
Step 2: Backstitch (1 strand)			
215		320	Pistachio Green-med.

42

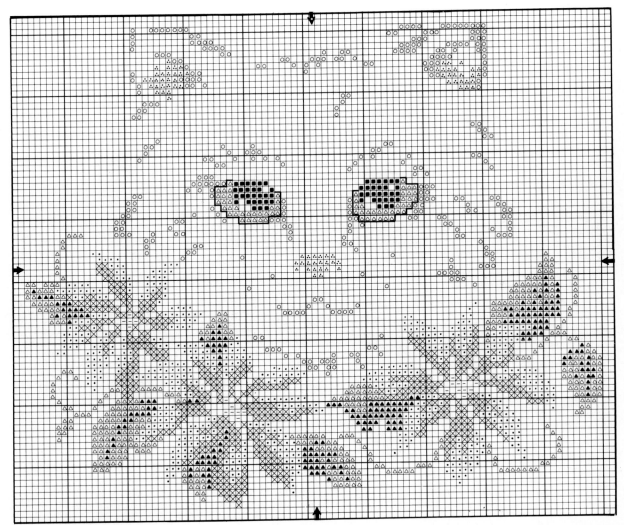

Stitch Count: 97 x 78

The ABCs of Christmas Garland

Bring words of good cheer to your home or a friend's home with a garland of greetings done in Christmas red and green.

MATERIALS (for about a 5'-long garland)

Ten 1½"-wide wooden star cutouts
Ten ¾"-wide wooden blocks
Ten ½"-wide wooden blocks
Fifteen ⅝"-wide wooden beads
Forty ½"-wide wooden beads
Drill with ⅛" bit
Acrylic paints: green, red, gold
Paintbrush
Three sheets of ½"-tall white vinyl
   adhesive capital letters (available at art
   and office supply stores)
Large-eyed needle
Red cord

DIRECTIONS

1. Drill hole through each star, block and bead as needed.

2. Paint wooden cutouts as desired. Allow to dry.

3. To adhere letters to blocks, peel desired letter from backing. Center letter on one undrilled side of block; rub down. Rub down same letter on the four undrilled sides of each block in desired phrase or word. Spell out seasonal words, such as Noel, Greetings, Santa Claus and Peace.

4. From cord, cut 2 yards. Pass cord through eye of needle. Make knot 5" from one end.

5. Arrange cutouts as desired, separating words with groups of beads, stars or smaller blocks; see photo. To string garland, pass needle through first garland item and pull item onto cord. Continue stringing, pulling each item back snugly against knot to make room for additional items as needed. When garland is completed as desired, knot cord at opposite end.

Try This

Letters may be stenciled on blocks. Use purchased letter stencils in desired size. Stencil letters in white as in Step 3. Allow to dry.

Stencils with holiday motifs are also available at craft stores. Or make your own stencils by tracing a design onto Mylar.

Using a craft knife, cut out the areas to be stenciled. Stencil the designs in the desired colors.

Cozy Christmas Button Pillows

Christmas colors, quilting and pretty buttons on crisp white make these pillows special. They're quick and easy to create, so you'll want several!

MATERIALS (for two pillows)

1 yard of white broadcloth; matching thread
2½ yards of ¼" cording
½ yard of fleece
Polyester stuffing

Red and green embroidery floss
Twenty assorted buttons
Dressmaker's pen
10½" x 10½" piece of muslin

DIRECTIONS (for red-stitched pillow)
All seams are ¼".

1. From white broadcloth, cut two 10½" x 10½" pieces. Also cut 1¼"-wide bias strips, piecing as needed to equal 45". From fleece, cut two 10½" x 10½" pieces. Cover cording with pieced bias strip; see "General Instructions" on page 126 for corded piping.

2. To make pillow front, layer one broadcloth piece, one fleece piece and muslin; pin. Using dressmaker's pen, mark pillow front with quilting lines; see diagram. Machine-quilt through all layers.

3. Using red floss, embroider feather stitch over long quilting lines; see "General Instructions" on page 126. Sew on buttons as desired.

4. With right sides facing and edges aligned, sew piping to pillow front; trim excess piping.

5. To make pillow back, pin fleece to wrong side of remaining broadcloth piece. Zigzag edges. Press to keep smooth. With right sides facing, sew pillow back to pillow front along stitching line of piping, leaving an opening. Turn. Stuff pillow firmly. Slipstitch opening closed.

DIRECTIONS (for green-stitched pillow)
All seams are ¼".

1. With remaining fabric, repeat Steps 1–4 of red-stitched pillow, randomly adding quilting pattern.

2. Using green floss, embroider herringbone stitch over long quilting lines; see "General Instructions" on page 126. Sew on buttons as desired.

3. Repeat Steps 4–5.

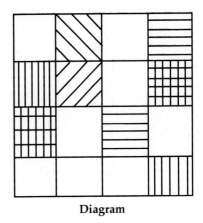

Diagram

Holiday Magic Embroidered Stockings

Heartfelt sentiments embroidered on country fabric express the true meaning of this special season.

MATERIALS (for three stockings)

⅜ yard of blue and white toweling
⅜ yard of white fabric
Tracing paper
Dressmaker's pen
Red and green embroidery floss

DIRECTIONS
All seams are ¼".

1. Enlarge stocking pattern on page 51; see "General Instructions" on page 126. Trace embroidery motifs and sayings opposite and on page 50. Place each tracing under stocking pattern before transferring to toweling. Plan open areas in toweling for design. Embroider flowers and lettering with red floss and leaves and stems with green floss as follows: Flower centers are French knots, leaves and petals are lazy daisy stitch and stems and lettering are backstitched. Using stocking pattern, cut out the three embroidered stocking pieces. Also from toweling, cut three plain stocking backs and three 1½" x 3¾" strips. From white fabric, cut six stocking pieces for linings.

2. To make one stocking, sew one stocking front to one unstitched stocking back with right sides facing and edges aligned, leaving top open. Clip curves; turn. With right sides facing, sew together long edges of one toweling strip to make hanger. Turn and press. Fold in half and tack inside stocking back at top, near back seam.

3. To make lining, sew two lining pieces together, leaving top open and an opening in seam above heel. Clip curves; do not turn. Slide lining over stocking, aligning top edges. Sew around top edges, securing hanger in seam. Turn through opening in lining. Slipstitch opening closed. Tuck lining inside stocking.

4. To make remaining stockings, repeat Steps 2–3.

THE LOVE OF
CHRISTMAS
IS FAMILY

Embroidery Pattern

THE MAGIC OF
CHRISTMAS
IS CHILDREN

Embroidery Pattern

Holiday Magic Stockings may also be made of velvet or satin and embroidered with metallic thread for a rich look. Use red seed beads to make the flower centers.

Embroider the sayings and flower motifs on a shirt or sweater to create a gift sure to be appreciated. The sweater can be a tiny one, made for a family pet! You can decorate a set of guest towels or cloth napkins the same way; they're perfect for giving or keeping.

Using these sayings as a guide, why not come up with your own heartfelt holiday sentiments? Or add a name or monogram to the pattern for a loving, personal touch.

THE DREAMS OF
CHRISTMAS
ARE FOR
EVERYONE

Embroidery Pattern

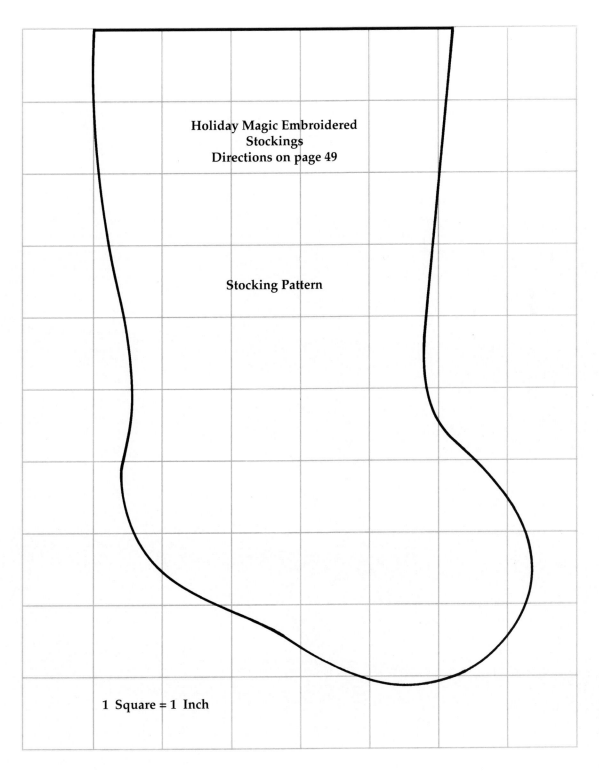

Holiday Magic Embroidered
Stockings
Directions on page 49

Stocking Pattern

1 Square = 1 Inch

51

Swinging Star Angel

This soft little angel will add the magical sparkle of Christmas to your home.

MATERIALS

Tracing paper
¼ yard of muslin
⅜ yard of red print fabric; matching thread
½ yard of green print fabric; matching thread
Polyester stuffing
10" of 16-gauge wire
Plastic beads
Acrylic paint: black
Pink blusher
Tape
Paintbrush
One package of yellow braided wool roving
Hot glue gun and glue sticks
1⅜ yards of ¼"-wide green ribbon
½ yard of 2"-wide gold wired ribbon
26" of 14-gauge brass wire
35"-long foil star garland

DIRECTIONS
All seams are ¼".

1. Enlarge patterns for dress on page 55 and star on page 56; see "General Instructions" on page 126. Trace patterns for body and leg on page 54. From muslin, cut two body pieces and four leg pieces. From red fabric, cut two dresses. From green fabric, cut two stars.

2. To make body, sew body pieces together with right sides facing, leaving opening according to pattern. Clip inside corners; turn. Stuff head and arms firmly with polyester stuffing. Bend 16-gauge wire in hairpin shape, taping ends; insert in body across shoulders. For wrists, wrap thread tightly ½" from ends of arms; secure. Fill body with plastic beads. Baste opening.

3. To make first leg, sew two leg pieces together with right sides facing, leaving top open. Clip curves; turn. Fill with plastic beads; baste opening. Repeat for second leg. Remove basting from body. Place tops of legs in opening, centering front and back seams. Slipstitch opening closed, securing legs in body seam.

4. To make dress, sew dress pieces together with right sides facing, leaving neck, armholes and bottom open. Make ¼" hem at neck and sleeves and 1" hem at bottom. Sew gathering thread around neck ⅜" below hem; do not cut thread. From green ribbon, cut two 19" lengths and two 6" lengths. Pin one 19" length around dress 1" from bottom hem, overlapping ends. Repeat with remaining 19" length ½" above first. Sew, turning under overlapping end. Repeat with one 6" length around each sleeve, 1" from hem.

5. Paint eyes on face. Allow to dry. Apply blusher to cheeks. Arrange braided roving in desired hairstyle; glue to head. Slip dress on angel. Tighten gathering thread at neck; secure. Tie wired ribbon in a double bow. Shape to resemble wings. Tack knot of bow to angel's back, stitching through dress into body.

6. To make star, sew star pieces together with right sides facing, leaving an opening. Turn. Stuff firmly with polyester stuffing. Slipstitch opening closed.

7. Shape brass wire into a 12"-diameter arc with a 9"-wide opening. Bend each end of wire into a hook. Cut 16" length of star garland; set aside. Wind remaining star garland around wire arc. Position fabric star so two short points span opening in arc. Sew one hook to tip of each point. Position angel on one short point. Sew in place; see photo. Bend one hand around wire circle.

8. Double 16" length of star garland. Twist strands loosely together. Shape into a halo. Place on angel's hair, securing with bead of glue if needed.

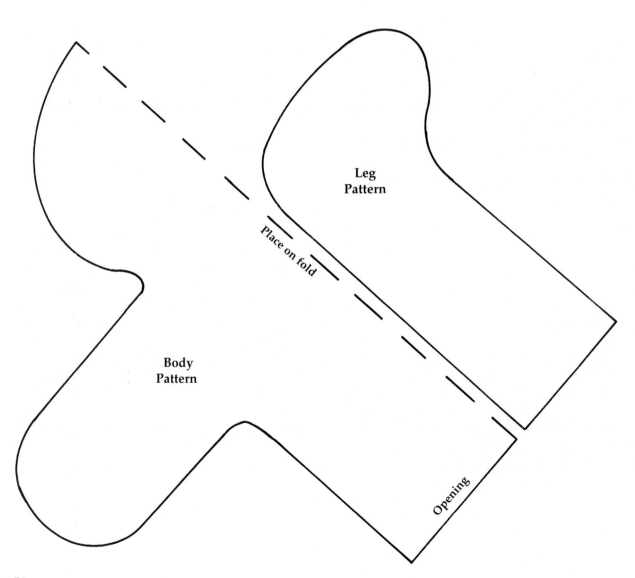

Leg
Pattern

Place on fold

Body
Pattern

Opening

54

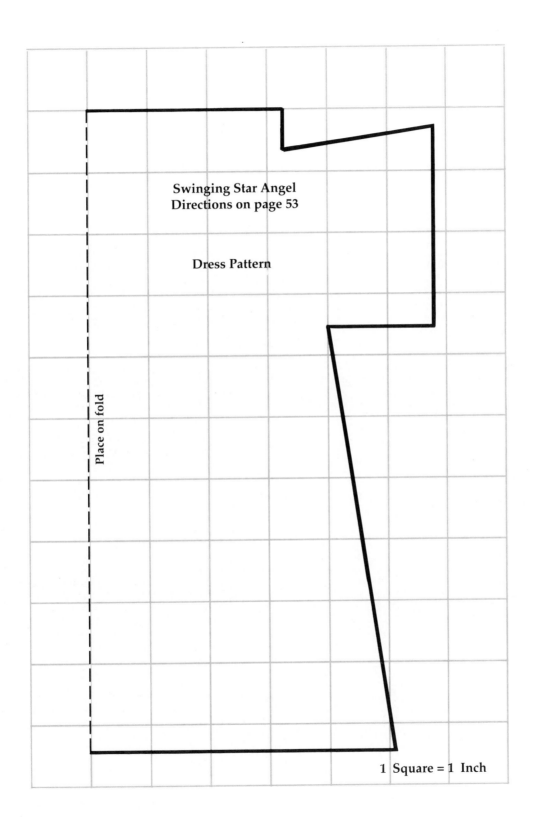

Swinging Star Angel
Directions on page 53

Dress Pattern

Place on fold

1 Square = 1 Inch

55

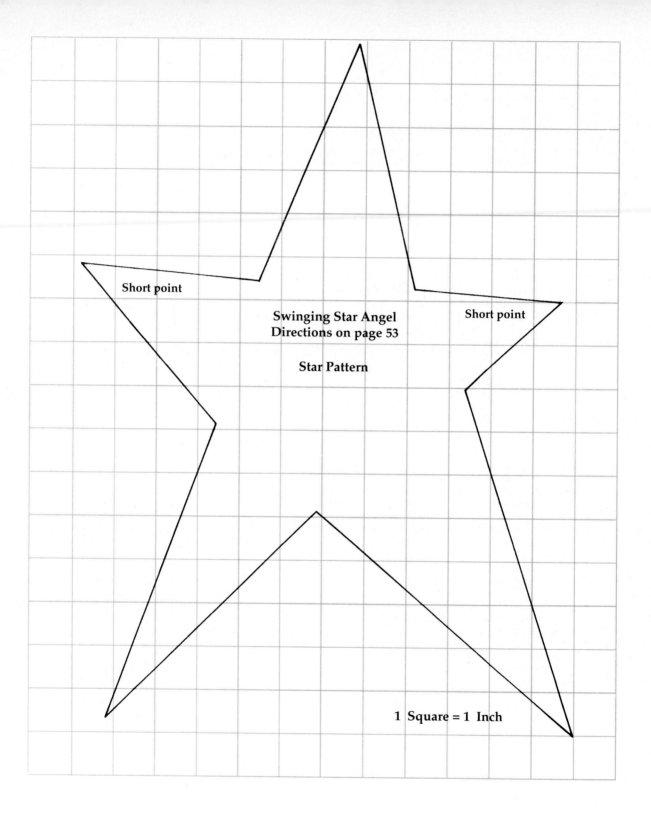

Short point

Swinging Star Angel
Directions on page 53

Short point

Star Pattern

1 Square = 1 Inch

Opposite: Christmas Country Pretzel Village

Christmas Country Pretzel Village

Create a pretty little snow-dusted country village with the simplest of materials, and nestle it among frosty pretzel pine trees. (Project pictured on page 57.)

MATERIALS (for one house)

11" x 11" scrap of bristol board
Craft knife
Pretzel sticks
Miniature shredded-wheat biscuits
Oyster crackers
Hot glue gun and glue sticks
Acrylic paint: brown
Paintbrush
Sheet moss
Imitation berries
Small dried roses
Cedar pinecones
Snow texturing medium
Craft snow or scrap of transparent
  plastic wrap

DIRECTIONS

1. Trace pattern for house side on page 59, transferring all information. Transfer pattern to bristol board; draw two house sides. Cut out. Using craft knife, score and fold along dotted lines. To make roof, cut out one 5¼" x 4" piece from bristol board. To find center, measure 2" in from one long side; mark. Score along center and fold, matching long sides. Set aside.

2. To make house walls, fit house sides together; glue. Using scissors, trim four pretzels to match height of house. Glue one pretzel vertically to each corner of house. Trim about 75 pretzels to 2½" lengths. Glue two rows of pretzels horizontally on each long wall with pretzel ends butting. Trim pretzels as needed. Glue one row of pretzels horizontally on each short wall, trimming pretzels as needed to match edges of gables.

3. To complete roof, fit folded bristol board piece to housetop; glue. Glue row of oyster crackers across one long bottom edge of roof, overhanging edge by ¼". Begin and end second row of crackers with a half cracker, creating a scalloped effect; see photo. Allow second row to overlap first row by ¼"; glue. Repeat with one or two more rows of crackers, aligning final row along roof peak. Repeat for opposite side of roof.

4. To make chimney, glue four shredded-wheat biscuits together in a square. Glue chimney to roof.

5. Using paintbrush, apply snow texturing sparingly to roof, chimney and house. Allow to dry. Paint windows and doors on house brown. Allow to dry.

6. Using scissors, shred scrap of plastic wrap. Embellish house with sheet moss, berries, pinecones, shredded plastic (or craft snow) and roses as desired; see photo.

MATERIALS (for one tree)

Twenty pretzel sticks
Hot glue gun and glue sticks
Scissors
Snow texturing medium
Paintbrush

DIRECTIONS

1. Trim pretzels to 2½" lengths. Group pretzels in pairs. Glue two pairs of pretzels together in a crisscross pattern. Continue crisscrossing and gluing pairs of pretzels on top of original pair until all are used. To shape tree, trim pretzels with scissors; see photo.

2. Using paintbrush, apply snow texturing to ends of pretzels.

─── *Try This* ───

To make larger or smaller houses, use a copy machine to enlarge or reduce the house pattern and roof pattern as desired.

To make a two-story house, double the height of the house side pattern's short edges. Add more windows as desired.

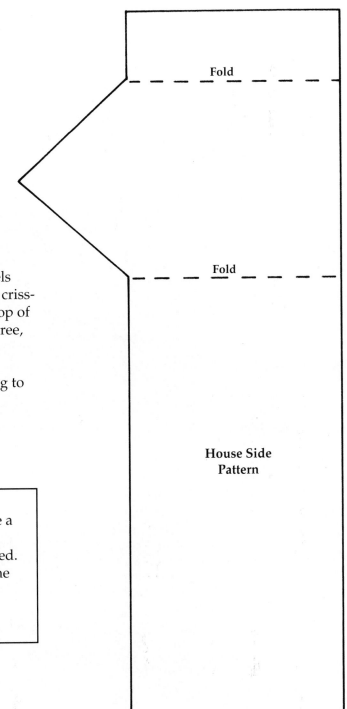

Fold

Fold

**House Side
Pattern**

ℐnowflake~Embossed Book Cover

Elegance in brass, this rich-looking embossed address book will handsomely complement every style of desk accessory.

MATERIALS

5⅞" x 8½" purchased fabric-covered
  address book
One 5¼" x 9" piece of 36-gauge
  tooling brass
Old scissors
One 10" x 10" piece of foam-core
Drafting tape
Extra-fine ballpoint pen
Blunt kitchen knife
1½ yards of ⅝" metallic or brocade ribbon
Hot glue gun and glue sticks

DIRECTIONS

1. Using a copy machine, copy tree and snowflake patterns on page 125 and star pattern opposite; tracing paper will not be sturdy enough. Using scissors, cut out one 5¼" x 5¾" piece and one 3" x 3" piece of brass. Tape edges of larger piece to foam-core. Center tree pattern over brass. Imprint tree outline on brass, using a ballpoint pen and even pressure. Position snowflake patterns as desired and imprint; see photo. Remove brass from foam-core.

2. Tape smaller piece of brass to foam-core. Outline star pattern with ballpoint pen. Cut out star with scissors; set aside.

3. Using blunt kitchen knife, carefully pry edges of inside front and back boards of book away from fabric cover. Center embossed brass on front cover; glue.

4. Cut ribbon into two 15" lengths and two 11" lengths. Glue one 11" ribbon vertically to cover, overlapping right edge of brass by ¼". Repeat with second 11" ribbon along left edge of brass; see photo. Tuck and glue ends of ribbons between inside front board and fabric cover at top and bottom.

5. Glue one 15" ribbon horizontally to cover, overlapping bottom edge of brass by ¼" and wrapping around spine and across back cover. Repeat with second 15" ribbon along top edge of brass; see photo. Tuck and glue ribbon ends between inside board and fabric cover at back and front of book. Glue all board edges back in place.

6. Glue star cutout to book cover at top of tree.

Star
Pattern

Christmas Comfort Appliquéd Pillows
Colorful painted clay miniatures decorate cozy country plaid pillows.

MATERIALS (for three pillows)

¾ yard of fabric for sashing and backing
⅜ yard of fabric for corner squares
¾ yard of fabric for pillow centers
⅜ yard of fabric for appliqués
Two 5" x 5" pieces of paper-backed fusible webbing
Tracing paper
Two 8" x 8" pieces of fusible tear-away
4½" x 4½" piece of fusible interfacing

Dressmaker's pen
Scissors
Polymer clay: white
Rolling pin
Wax paper
Large-eyed needle
Paring knife
Acrylic paints: white, green, red, yellow, black, brown, metallic gold
Red embroidery floss
Polyester stuffing
16" length of tan yarn

DIRECTIONS

All seams are ½".

1. From sashing/backing fabric, cut three 12" x 12" backing pieces and twelve 3" x 8" sashing pieces. From corner square fabric, cut twelve 3" x 3" pieces. From pillow center fabric, cut three 8" x 8" pieces. From appliqué fabric, cut three 5" x 5" pieces.

2. Trace appliqué patterns on page 65. For stocking and tree, transfer to paper side of fusible webbing. Place rough side of fusible webbing against wrong side of appliqué fabric. Iron. Cut out; remove paper.

3. Place shiny side of fusible tear-away against wrong side of pillow center fabric. Iron.

4. Position each appliqué, fabric side up, on one pillow center. Center vertically and place closer to bottom of pillow center to accommodate star stencil and clay miniatures. Fuse appliqués to pillow centers. Machine satin-stitch edges of appliqués.

5. For stocking cuff, cut a 2" x 2¼" piece from coordinating fabric. With wrong sides together, fold in half lengthwise; press. With folded edge at top, machine satin-stitch to top of stocking appliqué and pillow center, leaving top edge open.

6. For Santa's bag, cut one bag from appliqué fabric and one from fusible interfacing. Fuse interfacing to back of bag according to manufacturer's instructions. Machine satin-stitch around top edge above line indicating gathering string; see pattern. Position appliqué, fabric side up, on pillow center. Center vertically and place closer to bottom of pillow center to accommodate clay miniatures. Machine satin-stitch lower portion of bag to pillow center. Hand-sew two 8" lengths of tan yarn along gathering line till they meet in center; gather top of bag. Tie yarn in a bow.

7. To remove fusible tear-away from fabric back, lift at one corner and tear. To remove from appliqués, make small scissor cut in portion of tear-away backing appliqué; lift and tear.

8. With right sides facing and edges aligned, sew one 3" x 8" sashing strip to top and bottom edges of each appliquéd pillow center. Sew one corner square to each end of each remaining sashing strip. Sew one pieced strip to each edge of appliquéd pillow centers. With machine set at an extra-wide width, zigzag in-the-ditch around appliquéd pillow centers.

9. Work clay with hands until warm and pliable. Place clay between two sheets of wax paper. With rolling pin, roll clay until about ⅛" thick. Remove top sheet of paper.

10. To make clay miniatures, trace star, stocking, heart and gingerbread man patterns below; cut out. Place patterns on clay. Using paring knife, cut around patterns. Using large-eyed needle, make two holes in each cutout according to pattern. Bake clay according to manufacturer's instructions. Allow to cool.

11. To finish Christmas tree, trace star and trunk patterns on page 65. Using dressmaker's pen, transfer star to treetop and trunk to tree bottom. Paint star metallic gold and paint trunk brown.

12. Paint clay miniatures as desired. Allow to dry. Using red floss, sew to pillow fronts as desired; see photo.

13. With right sides facing, sew each completed pillow front to one 12" x 12" backing piece, leaving an opening. Turn. Stuff pillows firmly. Slipstitch openings closed.

**Stocking, Heart, Star and Gingerbread Man
Clay Miniatures Patterns**

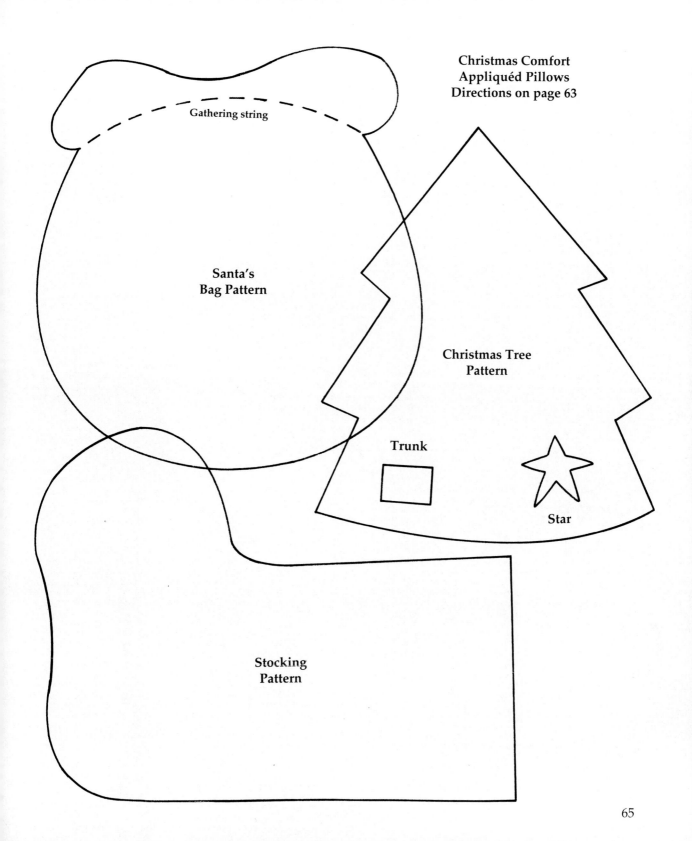

Christmas Comfort
Appliquéd Pillows
Directions on page 63

Gathering string

Santa's
Bag Pattern

Christmas Tree
Pattern

Trunk

Star

Stocking
Pattern

Happy Snowman Napkin Box

A simple box becomes a charming seasonal decoration with the addition of a jolly snowman, dressed up in a hat and a cozy, colorful muffler.

MATERIALS

1' x 1½' scrap of ¼"-thick plywood
9" x 6" piece of ⅛"-thick plywood
Jigsaw
Acrylic paints: light blue, blue, gray, white, orange, black
Sponges
Hot glue gun and glue sticks
Small brads
Hammer
Tracing paper
Spray adhesive
Clear glitter
Craft knife
Small chip of balsa wood
Six black seed beads
Five black wooden beads
Two 4½"-long thin twigs with hand-like ends
6½ yards of blue/green yarn

DIRECTIONS

1. From ¼"-thick plywood, cut two 6" x 6" pieces for box front and back, two 6" x 5½" pieces for box sides and one 5½" x 5½" piece for box bottom. Before gluing, check fit of sides and bottom. To make box, glue sides and bottom together; see photo. Nail small brads to box corners for reinforcement.

2. Sponge-paint box blue. Allow to dry. Using sponge, lightly daub box with light blue, gray and white to create the effect of clouds. Allow to dry.

3. Trace snowman and hat patterns on page 68. Transfer patterns to ⅛"-thick plywood. Using a jigsaw, cut out snowman and hat. Sponge-paint snowman back and front with white. Allow to dry. Sponge-paint hat back and front with black. Allow to dry. Place snowman on flat surface. Apply a light coat of spray adhesive to front of snowman. Sprinkle snowman with glitter.

4. Using craft knife, shape balsa wood chip like a carrot. Paint chip orange. Allow to dry. To make snowman's face, glue on orange chip for nose, seed beads for mouth and two wooden beads for eyes. Glue three wooden beads to snowman's front for buttons. Glue hat to snowman's head.

5. Glue completed snowman to front of box. To make arms, glue twigs to sides of snowman; see photo.

6. To make muffler, cut yarn into 11" lengths. Handling lengths as one, tie around snowman's neck.

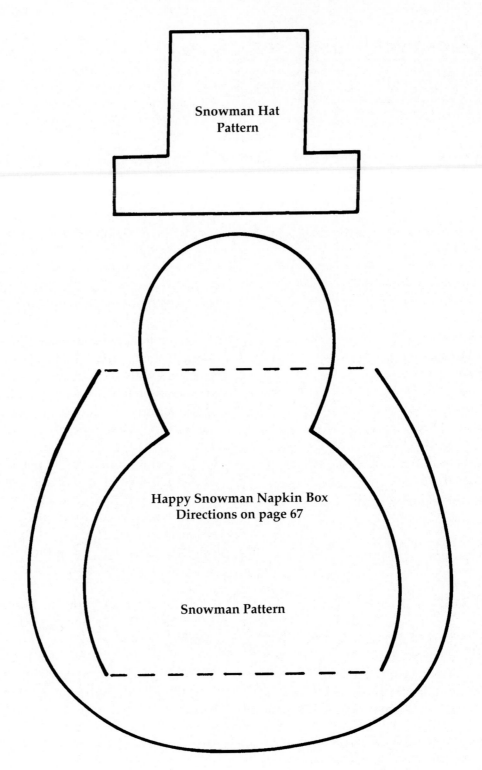

Snowman Hat
Pattern

Happy Snowman Napkin Box
Directions on page 67

Snowman Pattern

Opposite: Clever Cutout Place Mats

Clever Cutout Place Mats

Easy to make and easy to clean, these place mats in Christmas colors will brightly complement your holiday table decorations. (Project pictured on page 69.)

MATERIALS (for one red and one green place mat)

Two 18" x 12" pieces of red vinyl
Two 18" x 12" pieces of green vinyl
Four 20" x 14" sheets of paper-backed fusible webbing
Tracing paper
Craft knife
Manila folder
One 20" x 14" piece of mat board
Drafting tape
Ruler
Ballpoint pen

DIRECTIONS

1. Place rough side of webbing against wrong side of one piece of red vinyl. Iron. Repeat with remaining pieces of red and green vinyl. Remove paper.

2. With webbing sides facing and all edges aligned, place both red vinyl pieces together on a hard, flat surface. Cover with a towel and iron according to manufacturer's instructions until pieces are securely fused together. Repeat with green pieces of vinyl. Using craft knife, trim excess webbing from edges.

3. Trace heart and tree place mat patterns on page 71. Transfer to manila folder. Using craft knife, cut out one stencil each for heart and tree.

4. Using drafting tape, secure corners of red vinyl to mat board. Center heart pattern with top ¼" from top edge of vinyl. Outline heart with ballpoint pen. Keeping widest part of each heart ¼" apart, outline two hearts on each side of first heart; see photo.

5. Using craft knife and cutting through both layers of vinyl, carefully cut out hearts.

6. Remove red vinyl from mat board. Tape green vinyl to mat board.

7. Center tree pattern with top of tree ¼" from top edge of vinyl. Outline tree with ballpoint pen. Keeping widest part of each tree ¾" apart, outline two trees on each side of first tree; see photo.

8. Repeat Step 5.

Clever Cutout
Place Mats
Directions on page 70

Heart Pattern

Tree Pattern

Frosted Pinecone Candleholders

These pretty and practical candleholders are simple to make, and they'll add a cheerful glow to your holiday festivities.

MATERIALS (for twelve)

Twelve medium-size, upright pinecones
16-ounce box of paraffin wax
Two packages of red wax dye
Large, empty coffee can
Heavy saucepan
Metal tongs
Wax paper
Wire cutters
Twelve 3"–4"-long red candles
Metal spoon

DIRECTIONS

1. Place pinecones in freezer for three hours.

2. Place entire box of paraffin wax (about four sticks) in empty coffee can. Place 4"–5" of water in saucepan. Place coffee can in water and melt wax over low heat. When wax is completely melted, add wax dye and blend thoroughly with spoon. Lower heat just enough to keep wax liquid.

3. Remove pinecones from freezer. Use wire cutters to clip out top center of each.

4. Using tongs, dip pinecones one at a time into melted paraffin and dye mixture. Place dipped pinecones on wax paper. For richest color, dip each pinecone three times, allowing them to cool slightly between dippings.

5. Hold candle by the wick and dip ½" into paraffin and dye mixture. Quickly stand candle in top center of pinecone, pressing downward until candle is securely stuck to pinecone. Repeat for remaining candles and pinecones.

6. Using spoon, drip extra wax around base of each candle. Allow candles and pinecones to cool completely.

Try This

For a sparkling look, sprinkle pinecones with glitter while wax is still hot.

To make pinecone Christmas tree, dip pinecone in green-dyed wax. When cooled, place in small pot filled with sheet moss. Top tree with a wooden star cutout painted yellow. If desired, decorate tree with glass beads while wax is still soft.

When using lighted candles, always place pinecone candleholder in saucer or on non-flammable coaster. Always keep lighted candles away from flammable objects or surfaces.

Mr. and Mrs. Claus

Everyone's favorite Christmas couple, dressed in holiday finery, stands ready to offer your guests a warm welcome!

MATERIALS (for both)

Tracing paper
Two 12" x 15" pieces of mat board
Craft knife
½ yard of fleece
Spray adhesive
½ yard of red velvet
¼ yard of green crushed velvet
Scraps of black velvet
Scrap of black/gold fabric
Acrylic paints: desired skin tone, blue, black, brown, green
Paintbrushes

1 yard of ⅜"-wide black/gold ribbon
24" of ⅝"-wide gold brocade ribbon
12" of ⅞"-wide gold brocade ribbon
11" of ⅛" gold cord
Two packages of braided wool roving
Hot glue gun and glue sticks
Cardboard picture props (available at office and art supply stores)
Dressmaker's pen

DIRECTIONS (for Mr. Claus)

1. Enlarge Mr. Claus body and arm patterns on page 78 onto tracing paper, transferring all information; see "General Instructions" on page 126. Transfer patterns to mat board. Cut one body ⅛" smaller than pattern to make backing piece; set aside. Cut one arm, one head/jacket and one pants/boots piece. From black/gold fabric, cut one buckle; set aside. Reserve tracing paper patterns. Trace Mr. Claus hat pattern on page 77. From green velvet, cut one hat piece; set aside.

2. Lightly coat wrong side of tracing paper pants/boots and arm patterns with spray adhesive. Repeat with jacket portion only of jacket/head pattern. Press patterns to fleece. Cut out one jacket, one pants piece, one sleeve, one glove and two boots. Peel off tracing paper.

3. Coat unsprayed side of fleece jacket with spray adhesive. Press fleece firmly to wrong side of red velvet. Repeat with sleeve piece on red velvet. Repeat with glove and boots on black velvet. Cut out, making fabric pieces ½" larger than attached fleece pieces.

4. Using hot glue on back of fleece, glue pants to mat board pants/boots. Leaving top edge unfolded, fold remaining fabric edges to back, clipping curves; glue. Glue jacket to mat board jacket/head. Fold bottom edge of jacket fabric under; glue. Fold edges to back, clipping curves; glue. Glue boots to mat board pants/boots, folding top edges of fabric under and butting bottom edges of pants. Fold edges to back, clipping curves; glue.

5. For arm, use hot glue on back of fleece to glue fabric sleeve to mat board arm. Fold edges to back, clipping curves; glue. Glue glove to arm. Fold cuff edge under, butting end of sleeve. Fold remaining edges to back, clipping curves; glue.

6. Paint face in desired skin tone to within ½" of jacket edge. Add eye with blue and black paint. Allow to dry.

7. To make belt, glue 7" length of ⅝" ribbon across jacket at waist; fold ends to back and glue. Glue on fabric buckle. Use ⅞" ribbon to make boot and sleeve cuffs; glue ends to back.

8. Glue completed pants/boots piece to backing. Glue completed jacket/head piece to backing with bottom edge covering raw top edge of pants. Glue arm to jacket; see photo.

9. To make beard and hair, cut three 4" lengths of roving. Fluff out and glue to head and face; see photo.

10. To make hat, sew together long edges of velvet hat piece with right sides facing. Turn. For hat pom-pom, tightly knot remaining length of ⅞" ribbon over pointed end of hat; secure with glue. Glue hat to head, over hair. Trim with ⅜" ribbon. Fold hat down, securing pom-pom to hair with bead of glue; see photo.

11. Place cardboard prop on wrong side of remaining green velvet. Adding ½" allowance, cut out two props. Glue velvet to one side of prop. Fold allowance to opposite side; glue. Repeat with second piece of velvet on opposite side of prop. Glue prop to back of figure, positioning so figure stands upright.

DIRECTIONS (for Mrs. Claus)

1. Enlarge Mrs. Claus body and arm pattern on page 79 as in Step 1 for Mr. Claus. From mat board, cut one body ⅛" smaller than pattern for backing piece. Also cut one dress/head piece, one arm, one apron and two shoes. Reserve tracing paper patterns.

2. Repeat Step 2 for Mr. Claus, cutting out one apron, one dress, and one sleeve.

3. Coat unsprayed side of dress with spray adhesive. Press firmly to wrong side of red velvet. Repeat with sleeve. Repeat with apron on green velvet. Cut out, making fabric ½" larger than attached fleece pieces. Spray wrong side of black velvet shoes with glue. Glue to mat board shoes. Leave top edges unfolded. Fold remaining edges to back, clipping curves; glue.

4. Using hot glue, glue shoes to backing piece. Glue dress to mat board dress/head, folding bottom edge under and remaining edges to back. Clip curves; glue. Glue apron to mat board apron. Fold all edges to back except left edge, clipping curves; glue. Glue sleeve to mat board sleeve. Fold edges to back, clipping curves; glue. Trim dress hem with ⅝" ribbon. Fold ribbon ends to back; glue. Trim sleeve cuff with ⅝" ribbon. Fold ends to back; glue.

5. To make apron ruffle, cut one 12" x 1¾" green velvet strip. Hem one long edge. Sew gathering thread along opposite edge; gather into ruffle and secure ends of thread.

6. To finish apron, position ruffle under edge of apron; see photo. Glue. Glue gold cord along bottom edge of apron, over ruffle. Use desired length of ⅜" ribbon to make apron waistband and bow; see photo. Secure with glue. Glue apron to dress/head. Fold left edge of apron, ruffle and cord to back of dress; glue.

7. To make collar, cut one 6½" length of ⅝" ribbon. Sew gathering thread along one edge; gather into ruffle and secure ends of thread. Glue around neck, butting top edge of apron. Fold ends to back; glue.

8. Paint face and hand in desired skin tone. Paint eye with brown and green. Allow to dry.

9. Glue dress/head/apron to backing, with dress hem covering raw top edges of shoes. Glue arm to apron; see photo.

10. Fluff several 1"–2" lengths of braided roving to make hair. Glue to head as desired. Carefully remove string from a 12" length of braided roving, leaving roving tightly kinked; coil and glue roving on head to make bun; see photo.

11. Repeat Step 11 for Mr. Claus.

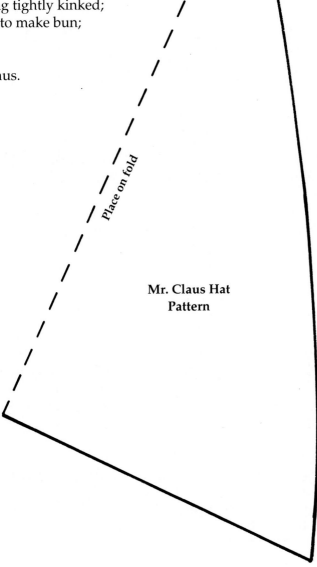

Place on fold

**Mr. Claus Hat
Pattern**

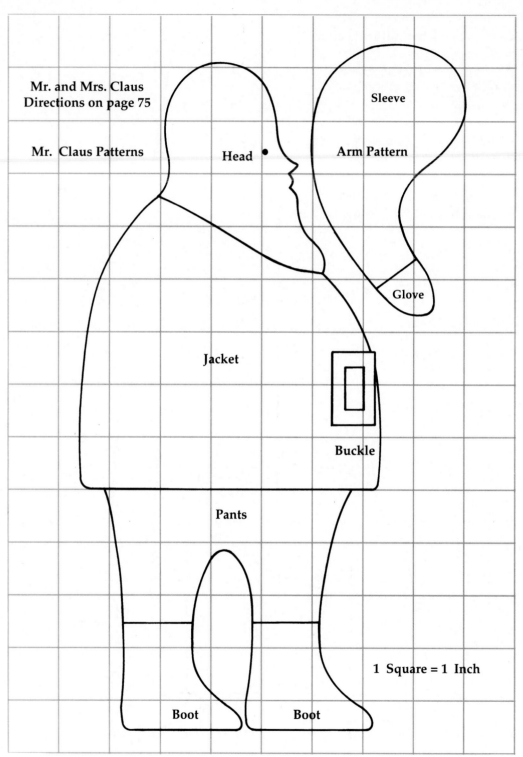

Mr. and Mrs. Claus
Directions on page 75

Mr. Claus Patterns

Head •

Sleeve

Arm Pattern

Glove

Jacket

Buckle

Pants

1 Square = 1 Inch

Boot

Boot

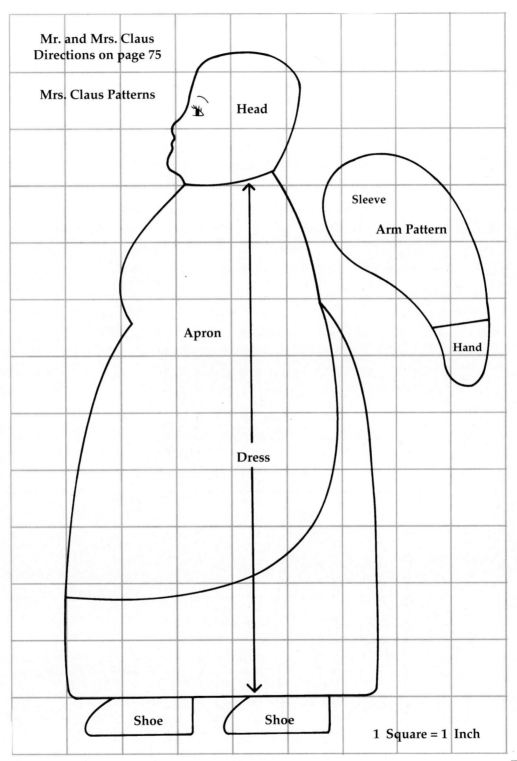

Mr. and Mrs. Claus
Directions on page 75

Mrs. Claus Patterns

Head

Sleeve

Arm Pattern

Hand

Apron

Dress

Shoe

Shoe

1 Square = 1 Inch

ittle Tree Clocks

The "holly" days are always busy; there's never enough time to do everything. These pretty Christmas clocks will help keep track of the happy hours!

MATERIALS (for clock with perched bird)

One 8" x 10" scrap of ¾"-thick wood
One 5" x 9" scrap of ⅛"-thick wood
3" of ¼"-diameter dowel
2½" of ⅛"-diameter dowel
One purchased wooden star cutout
Four small, wooden blocks
Small quartz clock movement

5½" oval wooden base
Drill with ¼" and ⅛" bits
Jigsaw
Acrylic paints: green, maroon, yellow, brown, black, ecru
Sponge
One sheet of medium-grit sandpaper
Hot glue gun and glue sticks

DIRECTIONS

1. Trace tree pattern on page 83 and bird patterns on page 82, transferring all information. Transfer tree pattern to ¾"-thick wooden scrap. Transfer bird patterns to ⅛"-thick wooden scrap. Also on ⅛"-thick scrap, draw a 3¼"-diameter circle and mark its center.

2. Using a jigsaw, cut out tree, bird and circle. Cut square hole out of tree for clock movement, according to pattern. Drill ¼"-diameter hole ½" deep in base of tree, according to pattern. Drill ¼"-diameter hole through oval base centered 1½" from top long edge. Drill two ½"-deep, ⅛"-diameter holes in center front of tree, according to pattern. Drill ¼"-diameter hole through center of wooden circle.

3. Cut ⅛"-diameter dowel to one 1½" length and one 1" length.

4. Sponge-paint tree green. Paint bird maroon with yellow beak and black eye. Paint star yellow and base and 1½" dowel length brown. Paint 1" dowel length green. Paint circle ecru with brown numerals and hour markers. Paint or stencil wooden blocks as desired. Allow to dry. Lightly sand edges of tree, bird, star and base for antique effect.

5. Glue wing to bird; see photo. Insert ¼" dowel in hole in tree base; glue. Install clock movement in tree. Position circle so clock hands will come through its center; glue circle to tree. Install clock hands. Glue green dowel into top hole in front of tree and brown dowel into second hole. Glue bird's back side to green dowel and bird's bottom to brown dowel; see photo. Glue star to top of tree.

6. Apply glue to dowel attached to tree and insert into hole in oval base; push it through so it is flush with bottom of base. Glue small, painted wooden blocks to base as desired; see photo.

MATERIALS (for clock with birdhouse)

One 8" x 10" scrap of ¾"-thick wood
One 5" x 9" scrap of ⅛"-thick wood
3" of ¼"-diameter dowel
Purchased miniature wooden birdhouse
Small quartz clock movement
5½" oval wooden base
Drill with ¼" and ⅛" bits
Jigsaw

Acrylic paints:
   green, maroon, yellow, brown, ecru, black, metallic gold
Sponge
One sheet of medium-grit sandpaper
Hot glue gun and glue sticks

brown; see photo. Paint birdhouse maroon. Sand one surface of circle smooth. Very lightly sponge-paint circle with gold. Paint numerals and hour markers in gold. Lightly sand edges of tree, bird, stars, base and birdhouse for antique effect.

4. Glue wing to bird; see photo. Insert dowel in hole in tree base; glue. Install clock movement in tree. Position circle so clock hands will come through its center; glue circle to tree. Install clock hands. Glue birdhouse, slightly askew, to flat top of tree. Glue one star to tree and other star and bird to base; see photo.

5. Apply glue to dowel attached to tree and insert into hole in oval base; push it through so it is flush with bottom of base.

DIRECTIONS

1. Repeat Step 1 for clock with perched bird, transferring dotted line on tree pattern for clock with birdhouse. Trace star pattern on this page; transfer two stars to ⅛"-thick wooden scrap.

2. Using a jigsaw, cut out tree, bird, circle and two stars. Cut square hole out of tree for clock movement, according to pattern. Drill ¼"-diameter hole ½" deep in base of tree, according to pattern. Drill ¼"-diameter hole through oval base centered 1½" from top long edge. Drill ¼"-diameter hole through center of wooden circle.

3. Sponge-paint tree green. Paint bird maroon with yellow beak and black eye. Paint stars yellow. Paint base, birdhouse roof and perch

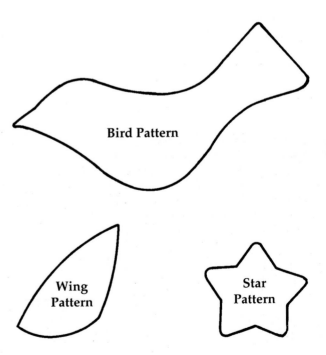

Bird Pattern

Wing Pattern

Star Pattern

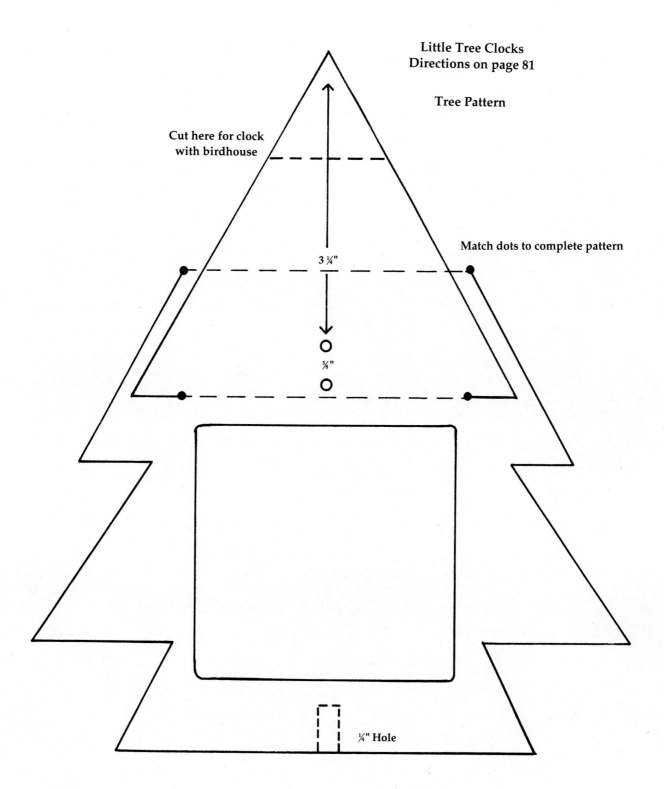

Little Tree Clocks
Directions on page 81

Tree Pattern

Cut here for clock
with birdhouse

Match dots to complete pattern

3 ¼"

⅝"

¼" Hole

Country~Fresh Napkin and Napkin Ring

Brighten a breakfast table with crisp checks and stripes. These cheerful napkins and napkin rings are ideal for keeping or giving.

MATERIALS (for one set)

16" square of green/red plaid
   fabric; matching thread
12" square of red fabric
Small amount of polyester stuffing

DIRECTIONS
All seams are ¼".

1. For napkin, hem edges of plaid fabric. Set aside.

2. From red fabric, cut one piece 4½" x 6", one 2½" x 11" and one 3" x 4½" for bow.

3. With right sides facing, fold 4½" x 6" piece in half to measure 4½" x 3". Sew raw edges, leaving an opening. Turn. Stuff moderately. Slipstitch opening closed. Set aside.

4. Fold 2½" x 11" strip with right sides facing and long edges matching. Sew to make a tube, leaving opening in center back and ends. To make pointed ends, mark seam ¾" from open end. Sew on diagonal; see diagram. Repeat on opposite end. Trim seams, clipping corners; turn. Slipstitch opening closed; press.

5. With pointed ends aligned, fold strip in half, forming an inverted V; press. Sew together 1" from fold. For bow loops, insert one 3" end of stuffed piece into opening and center, easing fullness on both loops. Tack each side of bow loops to tails as desired.

6. To make napkin ring, fold the 3" x 4½" piece, matching long edges. Sew to make a tube; turn. Fold in seam allowance on one end. Insert other end into folded end. Slipstitch ends together. Align napkin ring seam on back of bow/tails; slipstitch. Insert napkin in completed ring.

Diagram

Try This

For a holiday table, tack a sprig of silk holly to the middle of the napkin ring bow.

For an elegant touch, make the napkin ring from a rich brocade fabric and the napkin from a jewel-toned solid fabric.

$\mathscr{B}$eary Merry Kitchen Set

A merry (and practical) Mama Bear, a decorated oven mitt and a dressed-up towel make the holiday kitchen colorful and cheery!

MATERIALS (for bear towel hanger)

Purchased green
  hand towel
¼ yard of tan fabric
¼ yard of muslin
⅛ yard of red print
  fabric
¼ yard of flannel
⅛ yard of white/red
  print fabric
Scrap of dark
  brown fabric
Scrap of green print
  fabric
Thread: red, tan, green,
  dark brown
14" x 14" piece of
  paper-backed
  fusible webbing

½ yard of fusible
  tear-away
Tracing paper
¼ yard of ½"-wide
  white trim
⅜ yard of ¼"-wide
  green ribbon
⅝ yard of ¾"-wide
  white trim
Dressmaker's pen
One brown button
One miniature
  wooden spoon
Acrylic paint: red
Paintbrush
Small nail

DIRECTIONS
All seams are ¼".

1. Enlarge bear body pattern on page 92, transferring all information; see "General Instructions" on page 126. Trace arm flap, hat, paw, small tree and collar patterns on page 90 and bear head pattern on page 91, transferring all information. From muslin, cut one bear body. From tan fabric, cut one head, two arms and four arm flaps. Also cut two arm flaps from flannel. From tear-away, cut one bear body. Reverse bear body pattern and cut one bear body from tan fabric and one from flannel. Cut one hat from white/red fabric; set aside.

2. Transfer appliqués separately (bear head, nose, ears, paw, collar, bodice, two sleeves, two arms, eight trees) to paper side of fusible webbing, leaving ½" between each. Cut out, leaving space between each; do not remove paper. Fuse rough side of webbing sleeves, collar and four trees to red fabric. Repeat with bodice on white/red fabric and bear head and arms on tan fabric. Repeat with ears, nose and paw on dark brown fabric and four trees on green fabric. Cut out appliqués. Remove paper.

3. Sew gathering thread along one edge of ½"-wide trim; gather loosely. With right side of trim facing wrong side of collar, baste trim under bottom edge of collar. From ¾"-wide trim, cut two 5" lengths; set aside remaining trim. Sew gathering thread along one edge; gather loosely. With right side of trim facing wrong side of sleeve, baste one length under wrist end of each sleeve. Position appliqués one at a time on muslin bear body according to pattern; see photo. Fuse. Position trees ½" apart, parallel to and 1" from bottom edge of towel, alternating colors. Fuse.

4. From green ribbon, cut two 3" lengths. Sew one length across wrist end of each sleeve, hiding raw edge.

5. Place shiny side of tear-away bear body against wrong side of appliquéd bear body. Iron. Using dressmaker's pen, transfer bear mouth and eyes to face; machine satin-stitch with dark brown thread. Machine satin-stitch edges of ears, nose and paw with dark brown thread; satin-stitch bodice and collar with red. Satin-stitch edges of head and snout with tan thread. From tear-away, cut one 3" x 18" piece. Place shiny side against bottom edge of towel. Iron. Machine satin-stitch edges of red trees with red thread, green trees with green thread. To remove tear-away from appliqués, make a small scissor cut in portion of tear-away on back of appliqué; lift and tear.

6. Hem lower edge of hat by turning under ¼" and topstitching. Sew gathering thread along hemmed edge; gather loosely to width of 5½" and secure. Sew gathering thread along edge of remaining ¾"-wide trim; gather and sew trim close to gathered edge of hat. Sew gathering thread along top edge of hat; gather loosely to width of 5½" and secure. Pin edge to muslin body. Sew trimmed edge of hat in position on bear head; see photo.

7. Pin flannel arm flap to wrong side of one tan arm flap. With right sides facing, sew to second tan arm flap. Repeat with remaining flannel and tan arm flaps. Turn. Finish edges with machine satin stitching, using tan thread. To make hanger, baste flannel bear body to wrong side of appliquéd bear body. With right sides facing, pin together appliquéd body and unstitched body. Position arm flaps between the two according to pattern. Sew bodies together, securing flaps, top of hat and all raw edges in seam; leave bottom open.

8. Pleat top edge of towel to measure 4¾". With right sides facing, sew to bottom of hanger front, leaving bottom of hanger back free. From white/red fabric, cut one 2"-wide strip ½" longer than width of towel to make binding. With right sides facing and edges aligned, sew binding to bottom edge of towel. Fold binding double to wrong side of towel, turning ends in; slipstitch.

9. Make buttonhole according to bear body pattern. Button arms together. Sew button opposite buttonhole on back side of "paw" arm. Using small nail, make two holes ¼" apart in lower portion of spoon handle. Paint spoon red. Allow to dry. Sew spoon to arm between flaps. Close flaps around spoon; slipstitch tips together.

MATERIALS (for oven mitt)

¾ yard of red print fabric
Heat-resistant batting
⅛ yard of green print fabric
⅛ yard of white print fabric
Red and green thread
6" x 6" piece of paper-backed fusible webbing
Tracing paper
Dressmaker's pen

DIRECTIONS

1. To make mitt pattern, trace around a purchased oven mitt with vent, adding ¼" seam allowance. Draw four mitts on red fabric, two mitts on batting. Cut out.

2. Layer one red fabric mitt, one batting mitt and one red fabric mitt; pin. Machine-quilt 1½" squares diagonally across fabric. Repeat.

3. Trace small tree pattern on page 90. Transfer six trees to paper side of fusible webbing, leaving at least ½" between each. Cut out, leaving space between each; do not remove paper. Fuse rough side of three webbing trees to green fabric. Repeat with three webbing trees on white fabric. Cut out appliqués. Remove paper.

4. Position trees in two rows of three on mitt front, alternating colors; see photo. Fuse. Machine satin-stitch edges of green trees with green thread and white trees with red thread.

5. From remaining red fabric, cut 1½"-wide bias strips, piecing as needed to equal perimeter of mitt plus 5". From binding, cut two lengths to fit from corner below thumb to ½" above vent top; reserve remainder.

6. With right sides facing, sew one length of binding to wrong side of mitt front from corner below thumb to ½" above vent top. Fold double to right side and sew along stitching line of binding. Repeat with second length of binding on mitt back.

7. Place mitt front and back together with wrong sides facing and edges aligned; pin. Sew together. With right sides facing, sew remaining binding to back of mitt, beginning where raw ends of first binding lengths meet above vent top and leaving a 5"-long tail at corner below thumb. Turn edges of tail in; sew. Fold binding double to mitt front and

sew along stitching line of binding. Loop tail to back of mitt; turn end under and sew in place.

MATERIALS (for towel)

Purchased green hand towel
6" x 6" piece of paper-backed fusible webbing
Scrap of white print fabric
2" x 2" piece of red print fabric
⅛ yard of white/red print fabric
7" x 7" piece of fusible tear-away
Red thread
Tracing paper
Twelve green sew-on rhinestones
⅜ yard of ⅛"-wide red cord

DIRECTIONS

1. Trace large tree and star patterns on page 91. Transfer to paper side of fusible webbing, leaving at least ½" between each. Cut out, leaving space between each; do not remove paper. Fuse rough side of webbing tree to wrong side of white fabric. Repeat with webbing star on red fabric. Cut out appliqués. Remove paper.

2. Center tree on towel 5" from bottom edge. Fuse. Position star on treetop. Fuse. Place shiny side of tear-away against wrong side of appliquéd towel; iron. Zigzag lengths of red braid diagonally on tree, trimming braid as needed to fit. Machine satin-stitch appliqué edges with red thread, covering ends of braid. To remove tear-away, make a small scissor cut in portion of tear-away on back of appliqué. Sew on rhinestones as desired; see photo.

3. From white/red fabric, cut one 2"-wide strip ½" longer than width of towel to make binding. With right sides facing and edges aligned, sew binding to bottom edge of towel. Fold binding double to wrong side of towel, turning ends in; slipstitch.

Small Tree Pattern

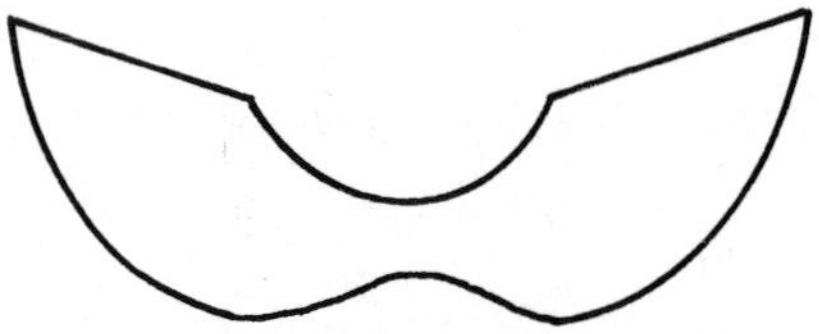

Collar Pattern

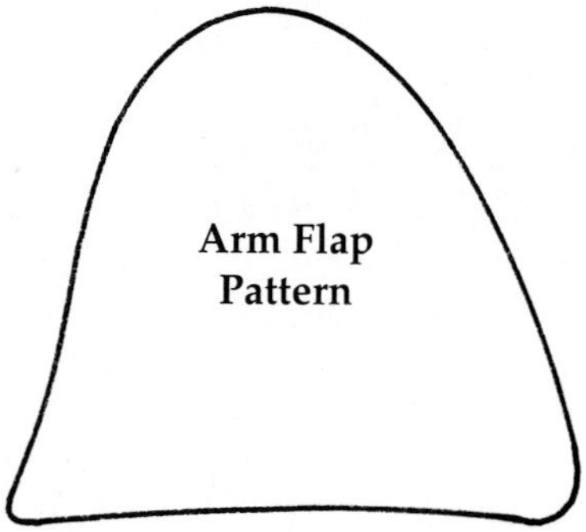

Arm Flap Pattern

Paw Pattern

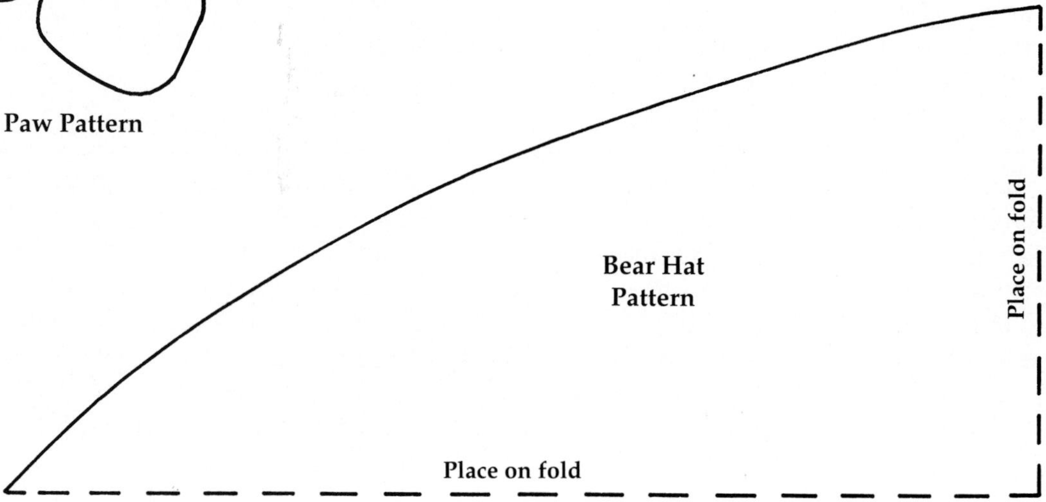

Bear Hat Pattern

Place on fold

Place on fold

Bear Head Pattern

Ear

Ear

Nose

Star
Pattern

Large Tree
Pattern

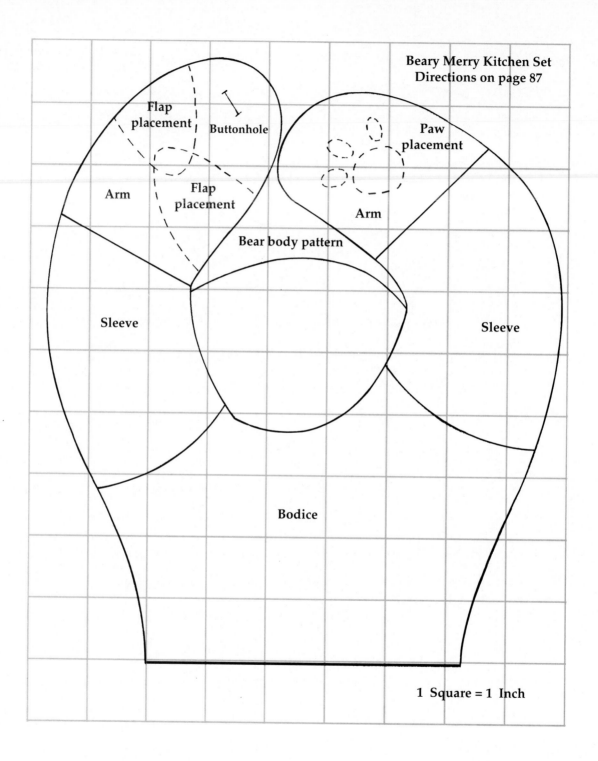

Beary Merry Kitchen Set
Directions on page 87

Flap placement

Buttonhole

Paw placement

Arm

Flap placement

Arm

Bear body pattern

Sleeve

Sleeve

Bodice

1 Square = 1 Inch

Opposite: Holiday Handkerchief Angel

Holiday Handkerchief Angel

This sweet and dainty angel adds beauty to your holiday decorations, and she's so simple and inexpensive to make! (Project pictured on page 93.)

MATERIALS

⅛ yard of cotton fabric; matching thread
Polyester stuffing
1"-diameter wooden bead
⅝"-diameter rounded wooden button
Paintbrush
Acrylic paints: white, black
Curly Craft™ (Mini-Curl)*
Pepper berries

Hot glue gun and glue sticks
11" x 11" handkerchief with holiday motifs
½ yard of white craft wire
¼ yard of white netting
Spray adhesive
Clear glitter
½ yard of ⅛"-wide white ribbon
15" length of fishing line

*Available at craft and hobby stores.

DIRECTIONS
All seams are ¼".

1. From cotton fabric, cut four 3" x 2½" pieces for legs, four 2¼" x 1¾" pieces for arms and two 3" x 2½" pieces for body. To make leg, sew long edges of two leg pieces together, leaving one end open. Turn; stuff moderately. Repeat with remaining two leg pieces. Wrap thread around each leg near closed end to make ankles; set aside.

2. To make arms, repeat directions for leg, using two arm pieces for each. Wrap thread around arms near closed ends to make wrists; set aside.

3. To make body, sew around three sides of two body pieces, leaving top edge open; turn and stuff moderately. Set aside.

4. To make head and neck, glue flat side of button to large bead. Paint both white. Paint eyes on bead black. Allow to dry.

5. To finish doll's body, fold in seam allowance and sew gathering thread at open end of one leg; tighten and secure. Slipstitch leg to closed end of body at one corner. Repeat with other leg at opposite corner. Fold in seam allowance and sew gathering thread at open end of one arm; tighten and secure. Slipstitch to right side of body ¼" from open end. Repeat with other arm on left side.

6. To attach head, sew gathering thread ⅛" below open end of body. Insert neck. Tighten thread and secure, adding beads of glue if necessary.

7. To make gown, fold handkerchief in half diagonally. Cut slit in middle of fold to fit head. Sew gathering thread around slit; do not cut thread. Place dress over angel's head. Tighten thread where neck joins head; secure. Cut 3" length of ribbon. Tie around neck to hide raw edges. Knot in back; trim excess.

8. To finish head, cut Curly Craft™ into short lengths. Shape each into a U. Glue to head at curve of U. Fluff. Glue pepper berries to hair to form a halo shape.

9. To make wings, cut two 9" lengths of craft wire. Shape into circles, twisting ends together. Cut netting into two 9"-square pieces. Fold one square around each wire circle. Tie netting ends of wings together; see diagram. Trim excess. Pinch wings into oval shapes. Lightly spray with adhesive. Sprinkle with glitter. Allow to dry. Tack knot in center of wings to angel's back.

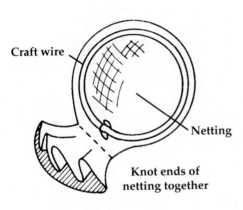

Craft wire

Netting

Knot ends of
netting together

Diagram

Try This

Angel body and legs may also be stuffed with fragrant potpourri to make a truly heavenly angel sachet.

For a truly elegant angel, dress her in a jewel-toned scrap of silk or brocade, using gold or silver cord at her waist. Glue sparkling beads to her hair. Make wings from brass wire and metallic netting or gold lamé; sprinkle with gold glitter.

Dress a country angel in gingham or in plaid towelling. Make fringed hem by pulling threads with tweezers around edges of fabric. Make wings from burlap; tie wings together with jute. Use jute to make waistband. Glue tiny dried flowers to her hair.

Make several angels into a garland by using colored ribbon to join them at the wrists!

10. Cut a 16" length of ribbon. Knot each end. Tie a bow around angel's waist, easing fullness of handkerchief over arms; see photo. To make hanger, thread fishing line through wings, making a loop; knot ends.

Little Brick House Doorstop

An ordinary brick will hold a door open, but a little brick house will do it in style!

MATERIALS (for one)

One standard-size brick
Acrylic paints: black, brown, white
Paintbrush
12" x 14" piece of mat board
Craft knife
Masking tape
Miniature plastic bricks (available at hobby stores)
Sheet moss
Assorted dried pink and red berries
Assorted tiny dried flowers
About twenty tiny pinecones
Miniature wreath
Hot glue gun and glue sticks

DIRECTIONS

1. Position brick on work surface with long, narrow side down. Paint windows and door black. Paint inside window frame brown. Paint window "glass" accents and doorknob white; see photo. Allow to dry. To make window boxes, glue row of plastic bricks below each window. Add a few plastic bricks to house front to give illusion of brick wall.

2. To make roof peak, use craft knife to cut two 2¼" x 5" pieces from mat board. Lay pieces end-to-end with short edges butting. Tape together with masking tape. Position taped pieces on top of brick and adjust angle so untaped short edges of mat board match short edges of brick. Secure mat board pieces with more tape, keeping angle.

3. To make gables, place taped, angled pieces edge side down on remaining mat board. Use as pattern to draw gable shape. Draw two gables; cut out.

4. Using masking tape, tape each gable securely to roof peak; see diagram. Paint completed roof brown. Allow to dry. Glue to top of brick.

5. Decorate brick as desired with sheet moss, pinecones, dried berries and flowers. Glue wreath to door; see photo.

6. To make upright doorstop, repeat Steps 1–5, positioning brick with short, narrow side down and adjusting measurement for roof peak pieces to 2¼" x 3" each.

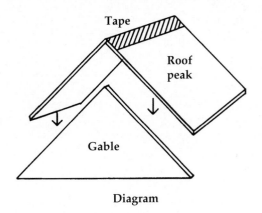

Diagram

tarry Forest Shelf Liner

Decorate a shelf with frost-dusted trees and stars. This copper shelf liner makes the most of the unique colors of patinated metal!

MATERIALS (for one 28"-long shelf liner)

15' of 14-gauge
  copper wire
Wire cutters
Tracing paper
Ballpoint pen
20" x 5" sheet of 36-
  gauge tooling copper
Old scissors
Newspapers
Steel wool

Paintbrush
Patina Green®
  finishing solution*
Soldering iron;
  soldering wire with
  resin core
Matte-finish acrylic
  sealant spray

*See "Suppliers" on page 128.

DIRECTIONS

1. To make shelf liner base, use wire cutters to cut 14-gauge wire into two 56" lengths and one 60" length. Bend each 56" length in half to equal 28". Bend unlooped ends inward. Handling both lengths as one, twist loosely together.

2. Bend 60" wire in half. Insert one end of twisted 28" wires through looped end. Begin twisting 60" wire snugly around 28" wires in a crisscross pattern; see diagram. Finish crisscross by wrapping ends of 60" wire securely around one end of 28" wire. Set aside.

Diagram

3. Trace tree pattern on page 125 and star pattern below. Place tracings on copper sheet and outline firmly with ball-point pen. Draw five trees and nineteen stars. Using scissors, cut out.

4. Place copper trees and stars right side up on surface protected with newspapers. Use steel wool to remove finish from surface of each cutout. Apply Patina Green® finishing solution with a paintbrush, following manufacturer's instructions. Allow to dry.

5. Solder trees along shelf liner base as desired. Solder stars along base as desired, soldering some stars to one another; see photo. Resin-core soldering wire needs no flux.

6. Place assembled shelf liner on newspapers. Dab finishing solution along base as desired. Allow to dry.

7. Spray shelf liner with matte-finish acrylic sealant. Allow to dry.

8. Note: Handle copper cutouts carefully. The edges will be sharp.

**Star
Pattern**

Band of Angels Garland

These captivating Christmas angels take flight out of your fabric scrap bag, sparkling with stars and ready to keep watch anywhere in your home.

MATERIALS (for one angel)

9" x 10" scrap of foam-core
Craft knife
Awl or drill with ⅛" bit
7" x 7½" scrap of print fabric
4" x 3" scrap of contrasting fabric
Spray adhesive
Hot glue gun and glue sticks
Buttons
9" length of tin star garland with five stars
Acrylic paints: brown, pink, green, white, red
Metallic gold paint
Black felt-tip marker
Dressmaker's pen
1 yard of ⅛"-wide green ribbon

DIRECTIONS

1. Trace angel pattern on page 102, transferring all interior features. Transfer outline of angel to foam-core. Using a craft knife, cut out. Punch or drill one hole in each wing, according to pattern.

2. Paint wings gold. Paint face and hands white. Paint hair brown and cheeks pink. Using marker, add details to hair and face, according to pattern. Allow paint and marker to dry.

3. Using dressmaker's pen, transfer angel dress pattern to print fabric; cut out. Transfer angel wing section pattern to contrasting fabric; cut out two wing sections.

4. Place angel dress right side down on work surface. Lightly coat with spray adhesive. Position dress on angel. Repeat for each angel wing section. Decorate wings as desired with green or red paint; see photo. Glue buttons to front of angel as desired.

5. Shape star garland into a halo, twisting the two ends firmly together. Position behind angel's head; glue.

6. Tie 12" length of ribbon through hole in each wing. Attach second angel beside the first, adding as many angels as desired. Use ribbons on each end of band of angels to hang garland where desired.

--- *Try This* ---

Reduce patterns to make smaller angels. Glue magnets on the back of each, and use as refrigerator ornaments.

Tin garlands are available at craft stores. Make your own by using a length of 18-gauge wire for a base. Twist wire into a halo, then glue purchased foil stars to it as desired. If you have a soldering iron, try this: Snip stars from tooling brass or copper, solder to short lengths of wire. Solder wires to the halo.

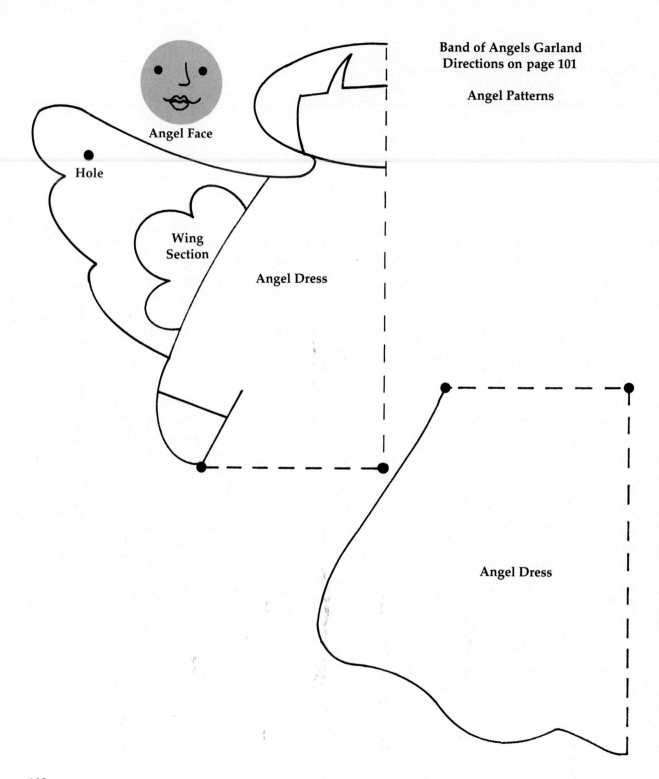

Angel Face

Hole

Wing
Section

Angel Dress

Angel Patterns

Angel Dress

Opposite: Appliquéd 'n' Stitched Stocking

Appliquéd 'n' Stitched Stocking

Satin stitching sets off a jolly Santa on this holiday-bright stocking.
(Project pictured on page 103.)

MATERIALS

¼ yard of green felt
Scrap of white felt; matching thread
½ yard of navy print fabric
½ yard of red print fabric; matching thread
Scrap of yellow print fabric
Scrap of white fabric
½ yard of paper-backed fusible webbing
½ yard of fusible tear-away
Tracing paper
Blue and brown felt-tipped markers
Three ⅝"-diameter black buttons
⅜ yard of ¾"-wide white wired ribbon
Powder blusher

DIRECTIONS

1. Enlarge stocking pattern on page 108; see "General Instructions" on page 126. From green felt, cut two stockings. From tear-away, cut one stocking. For stocking lining pattern, add 4½" to top of stocking pattern to allow for faux cuff. From navy print fabric, cut two lining pieces. From red print fabric, cut 2"-wide bias strips, piecing as needed to equal 1⅛ yards of binding; set aside.

2. Trace Santa stocking appliqué patterns on pages 105, 106 and 107. Transfer to paper side of fusible webbing, leaving at least ½" between each group. Draw moustache and beard separately. Cut out, leaving space around each; do not remove paper. Fuse rough side

of hat and jacket to red fabric. Repeat with beard, moustache, hat border and cuffs on white felt. Repeat with mittens and belt on navy fabric, face on white fabric and belt buckle on yellow fabric. Cut out appliqués. Remove paper.

3. One layer at a time, position appliqués according to pattern on right side of stocking front; see photo. Fuse. Sew buttons on jacket. Using markers, add facial features. Apply blusher to cheeks. Place shiny side of tear-away against wrong side of appliquéd stocking. Iron. Using red and white thread as desired, finish edges of appliqués with machine satin stitching. To remove tear-away, lift at one corner and carefully tear. To remove from appliqués, make a small scissor cut in portion of tear-away backing appliqués; lift and tear.

4. Mark line 4" below and parallel to top edge of both felt stocking pieces. With right sides facing, layer one stocking piece and one lining piece, matching top edge of lining to marked line. Sew ¼" from lining edge. Repeat with remaining stocking and lining pieces. Fold lining pieces to back side of stocking pieces. Layer stocking back, then front, matching all edges. Trim stockings and appliqués as needed to make edges even. Pin edges together.

5. With right sides facing, sew binding to stocking front, using ½" seam and folding ends under at top edge. Fold binding to stocking back and slipstitch, covering stitching line.

6. For hanger, twist white ribbon loosely and make a loop. Tack inside top of stocking back on heel side.

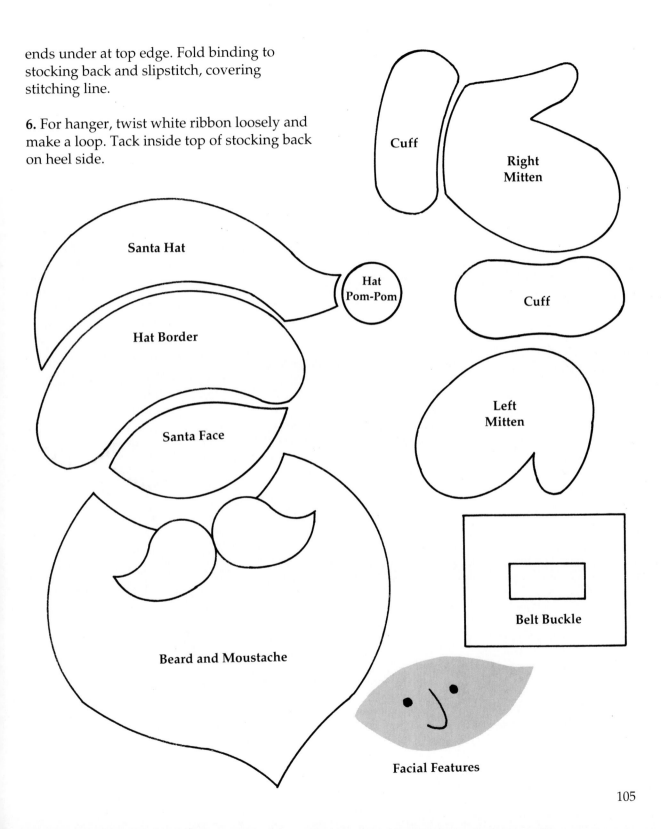

Cuff

Right
Mitten

Santa Hat

Hat
Pom-Pom

Cuff

Hat Border

Santa Face

Left
Mitten

Beard and Moustache

Belt Buckle

Facial Features

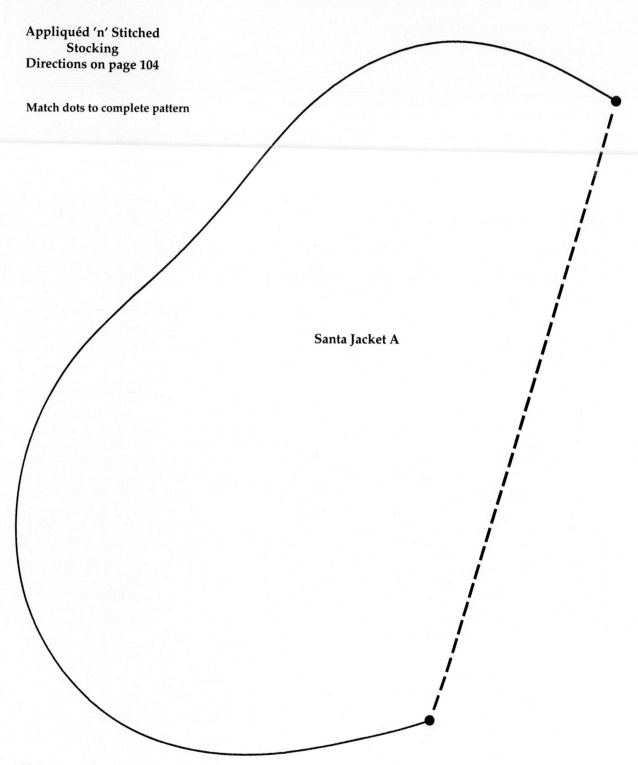

**Appliquéd 'n' Stitched
Stocking
Directions on page 104**

Match dots to complete pattern

Santa Jacket A

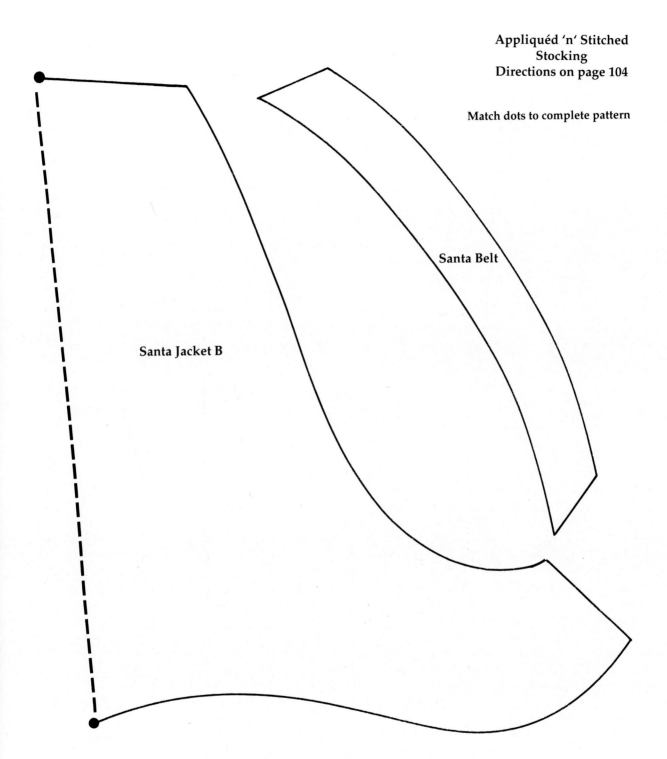

Appliquéd 'n' Stitched
Stocking
Directions on page 104

Match dots to complete pattern

Santa Belt

Santa Jacket B

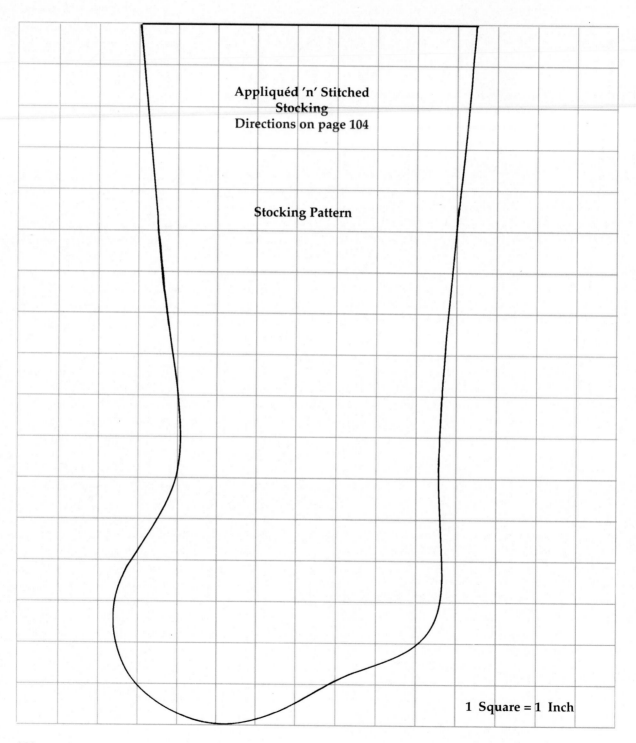

Appliquéd 'n' Stitched
Stocking
Directions on page 104

Stocking Pattern

1 Square = 1 Inch

Opposite: Stocking Stuffer Dolls

tocking Stuffer Dolls

With buttons 'n' beads and beads 'n' spools, create red-haired dolls guaranteed to bring a smile!
(Project pictured on page 109.)

MATERIALS (for boy doll)

Eighty ¾"-diameter
  buttons
Five ½"-diameter
  wooden beads
One 1"-diameter
  wooden bead
1¼ yards of white
  pearl cotton size 5
Tapestry needle
Paintbrush
Acrylic paint: black

Red acrylic yarn
Hot glue gun and
  glue sticks
Dressmaker's pen
6" x 10" piece of red-
  striped fabric
Two small, white
  buttons
13" x 3" piece of red
  print fabric

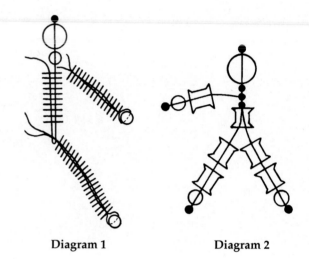

Diagram 1   Diagram 2

DIRECTIONS

1. See Diagram 1 for help with Steps 1–3. Thread needle with three to four strands of pearl cotton, making large knot at end. To make head and neck, pull thread through one large bead. Make knot and glue to top of head bead. Pull thread through one small bead. Wrap thread around small bead and pull back through at top. To make body, pull thread through one hole in each of ten buttons. Leave loop at bottom of body and pull cord back up through second button holes to neck. Leave end unknotted.

2. For arm, thread needle with three to four strands of pearl cotton. Pull threads through small bead until ends are even. Pull one end through one hole in each of fifteen buttons.

Remove needle; thread with other ends. Repeat through second button holes. Knot ends at neck. Repeat with second small bead and fifteen buttons. Trim excess threads.

3. To make legs, repeat Step 2, using twenty buttons and one small bead for each foot and passing thread ends through loop at bottom of body before knotting. Pull up loose thread at neck to tighten loop, securing legs to body. Knot loose thread at neck; trim excess.

4. Paint eyes black. Allow to dry. For hair, knot 2"-long pieces of red yarn; fray. Glue knots to head. Trim ends evenly.

5. Trace pants pattern on page 125. From red-striped fabric, cut two pants pieces. With right sides facing and edges aligned, sew together along center seams. Sew leg seams. Turn. Turn under ⅛" at waist. Using red yarn, sew gathering thread along waist, leaving 2" excess at each end. Sew two small, white buttons to front of pants; see photo.

6. To make shirt, cut two 4" x 2½" pieces and one 9" x 3" piece from red print fabric. With right sides facing, sew together short edges of larger piece; turn. Cut slits for arms. Hand-sew gathering thread ½" below neck edge. Slip tube over doll's head. Gather neck edge tightly and secure.

7. To make sleeve, sew together long edges of one 4" x 2½" red print piece with right sides facing; turn. Hand-sew a gathering thread at top of sleeve. Slip over arm. Gather tightly at slit in shirt and secure. Repeat for second sleeve.

8. Slip pants on doll, encasing shirt tail in pant waist. Tighten red yarn gathering thread at waist, easing fullness of shirt; secure. If desired, make hanger by sewing loop of ribbon to back of shirt.

MATERIALS (for girl doll)

Four ½"-diameter wooden beads	Acrylic paint: black
One 1"-diameter wooden bead	Red acrylic yarn
Seven 1⅛"-long wooden spools	Hot glue gun and glue sticks
1¼ yards of white pearl cotton size 5	Dressmaker's pen
Tapestry needle	24" x 5" piece of green print fabric
Paintbrush	10" x 4" piece of white cotton fabric

DIRECTIONS

1. See Diagram 2 for help with Steps 1–3. To make body and one leg, thread needle with three to four strands of pearl cotton. Make large knot in end. Pull thread through large bead, make two large knots, then pull thread through three spools and one small bead for foot. Knot ends. Trim excess.

2. To make second leg, thread needle with three to four strands of pearl cotton. Knot end at neck, above first spool. Pull thread through first spool, then through two more spools and one small bead for foot. Knot ends. Trim excess.

3. To make arms, thread needle with three to four strands of pearl cotton; knot ends. Pull through small bead and one spool; knot. Leave ½" slack, then knot thread at neck. Leave ½" slack on other side; knot thread. Then pull thread through second spool and small bead. Knot ends. Trim excess.

4. Repeat Step 4 for boy doll.

5. To make dress and apron, sew together short ends of green print fabric with right sides facing. Turn. Lay dress flat with seam centered in back. Center white fabric on front of dress, aligning top edges. Sew gathering thread ½" below top edges, securing apron to dress. Slip dress on doll. Cut slits for arms. Tighten gathering thread at neck; secure.

─── *Try This* ───

Use a variety of button sizes and colors to make the boy doll.

Stencil the girl doll's apron with motifs that complement the motifs on the print fabric.

Tiny Town Christmas Troupe

Six little wood and clay figures display six enchanting personalities. Let them add a whimsical note to your holiday decorations.

MATERIALS (for all figures)

Six 1" x 1¾"
  wooden blocks
One 3" x 15" piece
  of ⅛"-thick
  balsa wood
Craft knife
White polymer clay
¹⁄₁₆"-diameter bamboo
  skewer
Paintbrushes
Acrylic paints: gray,
  maroon, pink, red,
  blue, yellow, green,
  white, black, brown

Medium-grit
  sandpaper
Twenty-four ½" nails
Drill with ¹⁄₁₆" bit
Six scraps of lace trim
Hot glue gun and
  glue sticks
Gold thread

DIRECTIONS

1. Trace patterns for arm and leg on page 114. Transfer to balsa wood; draw twelve of each. Using craft knife, cut out.

2. Paint cat's jacket maroon with pink edging and pocket outlines; see photo. Paint remainder of body, arms and legs gray. Paint soldier's body, arms and legs blue. Paint braid and buttons on body yellow and stripes on arms and legs red. Paint feet black. Paint rabbit's body, arms and legs white. Paint vest yellow with two green Christmas tree motifs; see photo. Paint jester's body half green, half red; see photo. Paint one arm and leg yellow, one arm and leg blue. Paint feet black. Paint bear's body, arms and legs brown. Paint vest green with two yellow stars; see photo. Paint elf's body, arms and legs green. Paint jacket edging yellow; see photo. Paint feet brown. Allow all to dry. Lightly sand edges of wood to achieve antique effect.

3. Join arms and legs to bodies with one ½" nail each, allowing arms and legs to rotate freely. Drill ½"-deep hole in center of each body's top edge.

4. Sculpt heads from clay; see photo. Use blunt end of bamboo skewer to make eye holes. Use sharp end to draw facial features. Attach small oval of clay to each for neck. From bamboo skewer, cut six 1" lengths. Insert one about ½" into bottom center of each clay neck. If figure is to be used as an ornament, insert small pin or paper clip in top of head. Bake clay according to manufacturer's instructions. Allow to cool.

5. Paint cat's head gray with pink nose. Paint soldier's hat blue. Paint rabbit's head white with pink nose. Paint jester's hat red with blue ball. Paint bear's head brown with black nose. Paint elf's hat olive green with yellow ball. Allow to dry.

6. Put a bead of glue into hole in cat's body. Insert end of bamboo skewer protruding from neck of cat's head, pushing in until neck is flush with top of body. Repeat with remaining heads and bodies.

7. To make one collar, cut one 4" length of lace trim. Sew gathering thread along long edge. Place around figure's neck. Tighten gathering thread and tie at the back. Secure collar with glue. To make hanger, tie loop of gold thread around head of pin or through paper clip. Repeat for remaining figures.

Try This

To make a Santa figure, paint the body, arms and legs red. Paint the feet black. Use a red felt scrap for a hat and mohair scraps for hair and beard. For a belt, glue on a strip of black fabric with a gold paper buckle. Sew a tiny bell to the tip of the cap.

To make a reindeer, insert tiny twigs in clay head before baking. Paint body, arms, legs and head brown. Paint feet black. For a red-nosed reindeer, glue a red cinnamon candy to the nose!

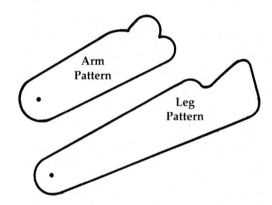

Arm
Pattern

Leg
Pattern

Opposite: Simply Seasonal Appliquéd Coasters

$\mathscr{S}$imply Seasonal Appliquéd Coasters

Simple, handsome and bright, these oversize 9" coasters are perfect for your holiday hors d'oeuvre party—a small plate and glass will both fit nicely. (Project pictured on page 115.)

MATERIALS (for four coasters)

½ yard of white fabric; matching thread
¼ yard of brown fabric; matching thread
¼ yard of green fabric; matching thread
¼ yard of red fabric; matching thread
¼ yard of yellow fabric; matching thread
One 12" x 12" sheet of paper-backed
   fusible webbing
Tracing paper
Scissors
Dressmaker's pen

DIRECTIONS
All seams are ¼".

1. From white fabric, cut four 9½" x 9½" pieces and four 6" x 6" pieces. From each remaining fabric color, cut one 6" x 6" piece and four 2¼" x 10" strips.

2. Cut fusible webbing into four 6" x 6" pieces. Fuse rough side of one piece of webbing to wrong side of 6" x 6" brown fabric. Repeat with green, red and yellow fabrics.

3. Trace heart, tree, star and reindeer patterns on page 117. Transfer reindeer and tree trunk patterns to paper side of brown fabric. Transfer tree boughs to paper side of green fabric. Transfer heart to paper side of red fabric and star to paper side of yellow fabric. Cut out all shapes. Remove paper.

4. Fold each 6" x 6" piece of white fabric in fourths. Mark centers with dressmaker's pen. Center reindeer appliqué on one piece, fabric side up. Fuse appliqué to white fabric. Repeat with remaining appliqués and 6" x 6" pieces of white fabric. Finish edges of each appliqué with lazy daisy, herringbone, running stitches or other decorative embroidery stitches in a contrasting thread color.

5. To finish reindeer coaster, sew four 2¼" x 10" brown fabric strips to reindeer appliqué piece with right sides facing and edges aligned. Miter corners; see "General Instructions" on page 126. Repeat, using green strips on tree coaster, yellow on star coaster and red on heart coaster.

6. With right sides facing, sew one 9½" x 9½" piece of white fabric to each coaster, leaving one side open. Turn. Slipstitch opening closed.

$\mathscr{T}$ry This

For a different look, use contrasting print fabrics for coaster borders. Patterns for appliqués may also be cut from colored mat board and hung as ornaments; just punch a hole in each and make hanger from ribbon!

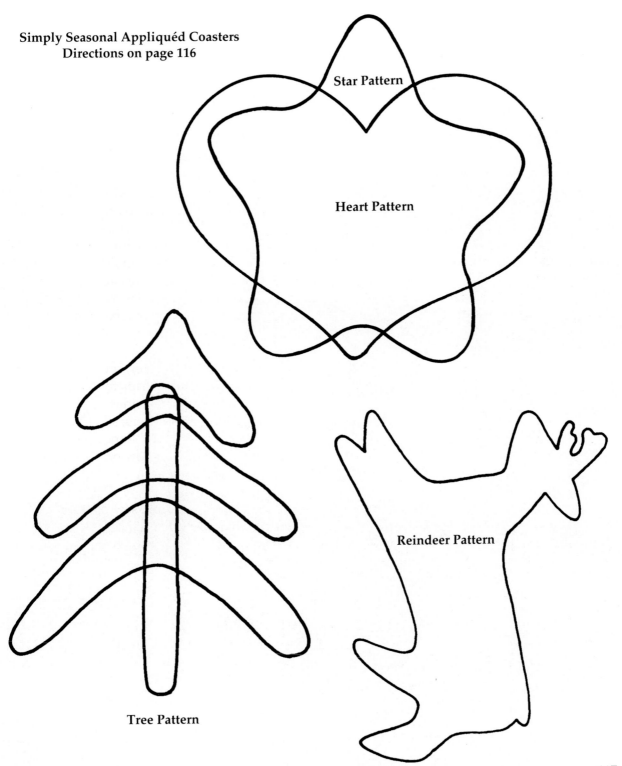

Simply Seasonal Appliquéd Coasters
Directions on page 116

Star Pattern

Heart Pattern

Tree Pattern

Reindeer Pattern

Marvelous Marbleized Ornaments

The colors and patterns of these ornaments are limited only by your imagination!

MATERIALS

Purchased wooden cutouts; see photo
  for ideas
Fine-grit sandpaper
Large aluminum pan
1½ gallons of liquid starch
Newspapers
Large plastic trash bag
Acrylic paints
One plastic cup for each paint color
Eyedropper
Toothpicks
Small squeegee
Small eyescrews
Gold cord
Assorted Christmas trimmings

DIRECTIONS

1. Sand wooden cutouts until smooth.

2. Cut one or two sections of newspaper into 2"-wide strips as long as pan is wide. Cover work surface with remaining newspaper. Place pan on newspaper. Cut trash bag open along one side. Spread flat beside pan.

3. Pour liquid starch into pan to a depth of 2". To remove surface tension, skim surface with newspaper strip.

4. Pour two tablespoons of one paint color into one plastic cup. With water, thin to consistency of whole milk. Repeat with remaining colors and cups. Fill eyedropper with one paint color. Holding tip just above surface of starch, float several drops of paint on surface. Paint should spread into a thin 3"–5"-diameter circle. If it sinks or blobs, it is too thick. Skim off with newspaper strip, thin and try again. If paint disperses quickly, it is too thin. Skim off, add paint to cup and try again.

5. Float new colors on top of first color and/or in pattern around it. Carefully rake *surface only* with toothpick to create patterns.

6. Holding one cutout with fingertips, slowly lower it so entire surface contacts paint evenly. Do not reposition cutout; that will destroy the pattern. Hold for five seconds. Carefully lift cutout and place, unpainted side down, on trash bag. Let paint set for 15–20 minutes. Gently squeegee excess paint from surface. Allow to dry.

7. For faded, antique effect, lightly sand painted surface of cutout. To paint other side, repeat Step 6. Decorate cutouts as desired with Christmas trimmings; see photo for ideas.

8. To make hanger, insert small eyescrew in top edge of cutout. Tie loop of gold cord through eye of screw.

Scent of Cinnamon Ornaments

A simple recipe creates two fragrant and durable ornaments. Make these two, then let your imagination set your limits!

MATERIALS (for cinnamon mix dough and angel and reindeer cutouts shown)

Large bowl	Tracing paper
½ cup of white glue	Cardboard
1¼ cup of ground cinnamon	Small knife
	Rolling pin
1 cup of boiling water	Wax paper
	Emery board
Plastic bag	

Note: Recipe makes enough dough for the two ornaments shown in the photographs on page 120 and 122.

DIRECTIONS

1. To make dough, mix glue and boiling water in bowl. Stir in 1 cup cinnamon; blend well. Knead dough thoroughly for 4–5 minutes. Seal dough in plastic bag. Let sit 1–2 hours. Do not place in overly warm area.

2. Trace small ornament patterns on page124. Trace angel and reindeer patterns on page 124. Transfer to cardboard; cut out.

3. Sprinkle rolling pin and wax paper sheet with cinnamon. Roll out dough on wax paper to thickness of ⅜". Place cardboard patterns on dough. Using small knife, cut out shapes. Punch holes according to patterns. Let cutouts dry 2–3 days on clean, dry surface dusted with cinnamon. Turn over daily. Cutouts will shrink about 20 percent. Use emery board to smooth any rough edges after drying.

4. If cutouts develop cracks, mix one tablespoon of cinnamon and one teaspoon of glue with enough boiling water to make thin paste. Use paste to fill and smooth over cracks. Allow to dry thoroughly.

MATERIALS (for angel ornament)

Cinnamon mix cutout	Six large bay leaves
Four cinnamon sticks	Hot glue gun and glue sticks
¼ yard of jute	
1 yard of brown cord	
Twenty tiny cedar pinecones	
Twenty-four dried cranberries	
Four whole cloves	

DIRECTIONS

1. To make leg, loop length of cord through appropriate hole on angel cutout and through one cinnamon stick; glue end securely. Repeat for other leg and for one arm. Tie small ornaments to brown cord and attach to knot at end of other arm. Make four small jute knots and glue one to each appendage end; trim excess next to knots.

2. Glue pinecones along bottom front of cutout. Use four cloves for buttons. Glue double row of cranberries around head for hair. To make wings, glue three bay leaves in a fan pattern to each side of cutout back; see photo.

3. To make hanger, glue loop of brown cord or jute to back of cutout.

MATERIALS (for reindeer ornament)

Cinnamon mix cutout; see directions for dough and cutouts on page 121
Four cinnamon sticks
¼ yard of jute
½ yard of brown cord
One whole clove
Two small twigs
Pepper berries
Hot glue gun and glue sticks
½ yard of ⅛"-wide green ribbon
Miniature gold bell

DIRECTIONS

1. Repeat Step 1 of angel, using four cinnamon sticks for legs.

2. For antlers, glue small twigs to back of head between ears. Glue one clove to head for eye.

---- *Try This* ----

Here's a way to make sure that your cinnamon mix dough is rolled out flat and even! Place the dough on the wax paper. Place one ⅜"-diameter dowel on the wax paper next to the dough. Place a second dowel on the wax paper, opposite the first dowel. Roll out the dough, rolling over the dowels. The dowels ensure a flat, even surface.

To make other cutouts, use different cookie-cutter shapes or trace simple decorative shapes from magazine pictures. Transfer the traced outlines to cardboard and cut out to create your patterns. Then repeat Steps 3–4 of the cinnamon mix dough recipe on page 121.

3. To decorate reindeer's neck, cut green ribbon into one 10" length and one 8" length. Tie bell in middle of 10" length. Thread ribbon through hole in reindeer's back, then tie around neck. Make a bow; knot ribbon ends. Glue cluster of pepper berries on bow as desired; see photo.

4. To make hanger, tie 8" ribbon length into a loop. Glue to back of reindeer.

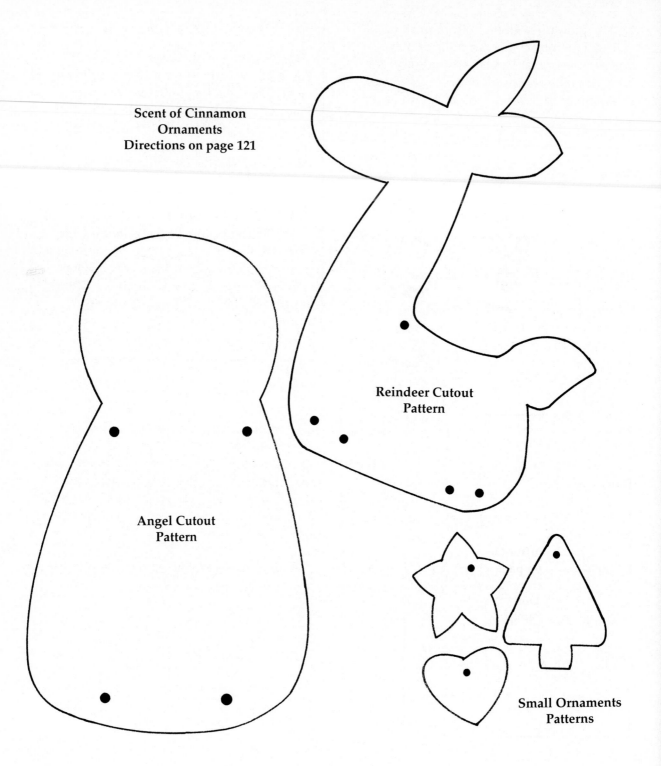

Scent of Cinnamon
Ornaments
Directions on page 121

Reindeer Cutout
Pattern

Angel Cutout
Pattern

Small Ornaments
Patterns

124

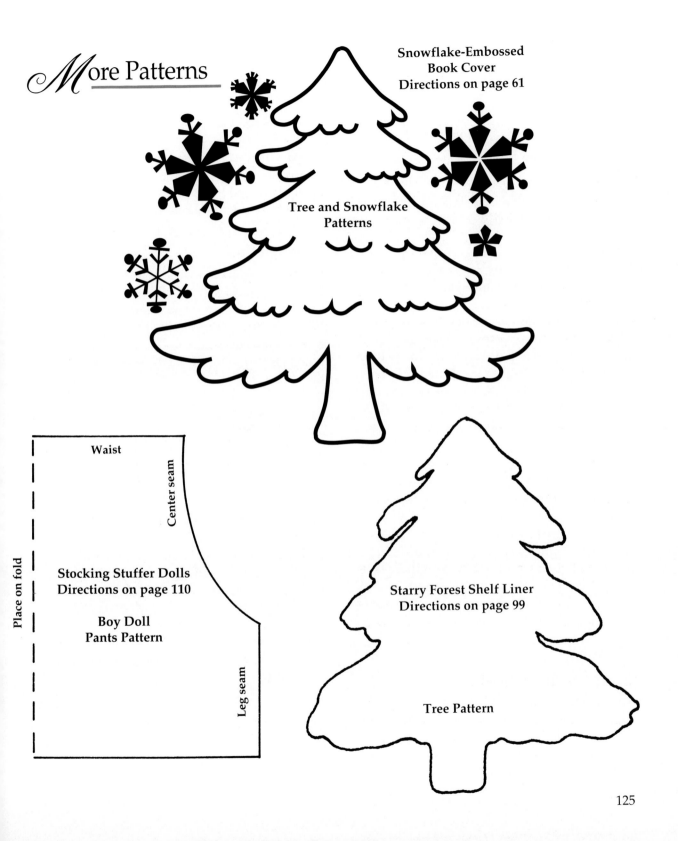

*M*ore Patterns

**Snowflake-Embossed
Book Cover
Directions on page 61**

**Tree and Snowflake
Patterns**

Waist

Center seam

Place on fold

**Stocking Stuffer Dolls
Directions on page 110**

**Boy Doll
Pants Pattern**

Leg seam

**Starry Forest Shelf Liner
Directions on page 99**

Tree Pattern

$\mathcal{G}$eneral Instructions

Easy Reference Features

Materials: The Materials List identifies the items used and the quantity needed to finish the model shown in the photograph.

Directions: The directions offer step-by-step guidance for completing the model shown in the photograph, plus helpful hints.

Transferring Patterns: Use tracing paper or Mylar to trace the patterns. Transfer all information. For projects requiring sewing, the patterns include a ¼" seam allowance. Patterns to be transferred to fusible webbing are printed reversed; when fused and turned, they will be correct. Patterns not printed with their project are on page 125.

Enlarging Patterns: Patterns too large for the page are prepared on a grid in which each square is equal to 1" on the finished pattern. To enlarge a pattern, use paper large enough for the finished pattern size. Mark grid lines 1" apart to fill the paper. Mark dots on these lines corresponding to the pattern. Connect the dots. Fabric stores supply paper with dots preprinted at 1" intervals. You may also use a copy machine or 1" graph paper.

Cross-Stitch Guidelines

The symbols on the graph each represent a different color. Refer to the code to verify which color and stitch to use. The code also indicates the brand of floss used to stitch the model, as well as the cross-reference for using another

brand. Use the number of floss strands called for. The symbols on the code match the graph. A symbol under a diagonal line indicates a half cross-stitch; see "Stitches" on the next page.

Sewing Hints

Corded Piping: Piece bias strips together to equal the required length. Place the cording in the center of the wrong side of the bias strip. Fold bias strip over, aligning raw edges. Using a zipper foot, sew close to the cording through both layers of fabric. Trim the seam allowance to ¼".

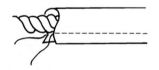

Mitering Corners: Mitering adds a crisp finish to corners on borders and bindings. Mitered borders have diagonal seams in the corner. To miter a corner, sew up to, but not through, the seam allowance; back tack. Repeat on all four edges, making all seams meet exactly at the corners. Fold two adjacent border pieces together as shown in the diagram. Mark, then sew at a 45-degree angle. Trim the seam allowance to ¼".

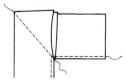

Tassels: Wind fiber around cardboard rectangle as many times as desired; see Diagram A. Secure bundle with strand of fiber; see Diagram B. Cut wound strands opposite tie; see Diagram C. Tightly wrap a single strand around bundle about one-third of the way down; see Diagram D. Tie ends. Push ends into tassel to hide them. Trim tassel to desired length.

Craft Hints

Wooden Projects: After cutting out all pieces and before painting or decorating them, assemble wooden projects "dry" (without glue) to check for fit and appearance. Drafting tape may be used to hold the wooden pieces temporarily in place. Paint, decorate and glue only after making any necessary adjustments.

Polymer Clay: The complete generic name is oven-fired polymer clay or modeling medium. Common brand names are Fimo, Sculpey and Cernit. The "Tiny Town Christmas Troupe" figures have heads made from Sculpey. For best results, work the clay with your hands until it is warm and pliable before cutting or sculpting with it.

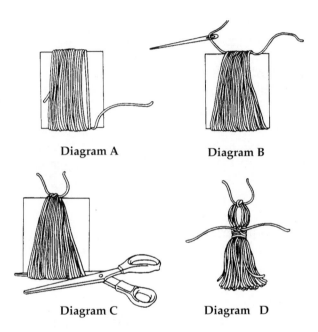

| Diagram A | Diagram B |

Diagram C   Diagram D

Stitches

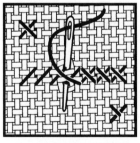

Cross-Stitch and Half Cross-Stitch

French Knot

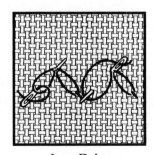

Lazy Daisy

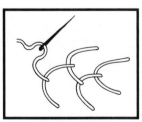

Feather Stitch

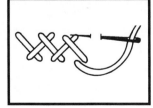

Herringbone Stitch

uppliers

For a merchant near you, write to one of the suppliers below.

Waste Canvas 10
Charles Craft
P.O. Box 1049
Laurinburg NC 28353

Polyester stuffing
Fleece
Fairfield Processing Corporation
88 Rose Hill Avenue
P.O. Drawer 1157
Danbury CT 06810

Patina Green® finishing solution
Modern Options Inc.
217 Second Street
San Francisco CA 94105

Acrylic paints
Delta Technical Coatings, Inc.
2550 Pellissier Place
Whittier CA 90601

Murano 30
Floba 25
Zweigart/Joan Toggitt Ltd.
Weston Canal Plaza, 35 Fairfield Place
West Caldwell NJ 07006

Red and black seed beads
Mill Hill division of Gay Bowles Sales, Inc.
P.O. Box 1060
Janesville WI 53547

Glue
Aleene's
A Division of Artis, Inc.
85 Industrial Way
Buellton CA 93427

Sewing machine
Bernina of America
3500 Thayer Court
Aurora IL 60504-6182